The Memoirs of Ludwik Żychliński

Reminiscences of the American Civil War, Siberia, and Poland

Translated by
Eugene Podraza

Edited with an Introduction by
James S. Pula

EAST EUROPEAN MONOGRAPHS
DISTRIBUTED BY COLUMBIA UNIVERSITY PRESS

1993

EAST EUROPEAN MONOGRAPHS, NO. CCCXCII

Dedicated to the Memory of all Poles
Who Fought "For Your Freedom and Ours."

Contents

Acknowledgement

Without the assistance of several people and institutions the publication of an English-language translation of Ludwik Żychliński's memoirs would not have been possible. The translator is particularly indebted to his wife, Krystyna Podraza, who lent invaluable assistance with the translation of obscure Polish words and colloquial expressions.

The editor wishes to express his gratitude to Dr. Richard Sommers and the staff of the U.S. Army Military History Institute, the National Archives, Dr. M. B. Biskupski, and the Adjutant General's Office of the Commonwealth of Massachusetts.

Introduction

Born in 1837 into a gentry family in the Duchy of Poznań, Wielkopolska [Great Poland],[1] Ludwik Żychliński grew up in a nation whose
political existence had ceased with the Third Partition of Poland in 1795.
During the forty-two years between the dismemberment of his homeland
and his birth, Poles fought valiantly but vainly to regain their national
existence under the banners of Napoleon Bonaparte and in the ill-fated
November Insurrection of 1830-31. Despite these failures, and the
occupation of their country for more than four decades, Żychliński grew
up in an atmosphere that deeply valued the preservation of Polish culture, where underground movements constantly intrigued and planned
for the day that a new revolution would bring national independence.

Ingrained with a love for freedom and the ideals of patriotic revolution, the youthful Pole migrated to Italy where he served in the Papal
Army before the ideals of national freedom drew him to participate in
Giuseppi Garibaldi's campaign in Sicily in 1860.[2] With the failure of
that movement, he journeyed across the sea to the United States, landing
in New York aboard the ship *Hemisphere* in April, 1862.[3] Arriving as

---

[1]*Wielka Encyclopedia Powszechna PWN* (Warszawa: Państwowe Wydawnictwo
Naukowe, 1969), Vol. 12, p. 870; S. Kieniewicz, T. Kopriejewa and J. Sztakelberg,
eds., *Zarys Powstania Styczniowego Opracowany w Warszawskiej Cytadeli* (Wrocław:
Zakład Narodowy im. Ossolińskich, 1985), p. 449; S. Kieniewicz and I. Miller, eds.,
Prasa Tajna z lat 1861-1864 (Wrocław: Zakład Narodowy im. Ossolińskich, 1966), p.
623; S. Orgelbrand, *Encyklopedja Powszechna* (Warszawa: Wydawnictwo Towarzystwa
Akcyjnego, 1904), p. 231 indicates Zychliński served in the Prussian Army.

[2]*Wielka Encyclopedia*, Vol. 12, p. 870; both Kieniewicz, et al., *Zarys Powstania
Styczniowego,* p. 449, and Kieniewicz and I. Miller, *Prasa Tajna,* indicate he served in
the Papal Army.

[3]The manifest of the ship *Hemisphere* on file in the National Archives lists "Louis
Zychlinski" as a passenger arriving in New York from Liverpool on April 17, 1862.

the nation began its second year of Civil War, he enlist in the Northern Army where he hoped to fight against slavery while at the same time gaining valuable military experience that could later be used in the struggle to free his homeland from foreign domination. The regimental descriptive book of *"Les Enfans Perdu,"* officially known as the Independent Battalion of New York Volunteer Light Infantry, indicates that he enrolled for three years or the duration of the war in Company E as 5th Sergeant under the name of "Louis de Zychlinski" on April 18, 1862. He was transferred to the rank of Sergeant in Company B on April 26 of the same year, but is thereafter listed as a Private.[4]

Following its muster in, Żychliński's unit was transferred to Gloucester, Virginia, where it was assigned to the defenses of Yorktown as an unattached regiment in the Fourth Army Corps.[5] In this capacity it served during General George McClellan's Peninsula Campaign in the spring and summer of 1862. Once in the army the Pole gravitated toward the faction supporting McClellan, whose charismatic personality cast a spell on many of his subordinates. Despite repeated defeats and obvious failures in leadership, Żychliński and others nevertheless defended the commanding general without question. Embittered by the defeats, the corruption rampant in the selection of officers and procurement of supplies, the human losses, and the rising tide of criticism leveled at McClellan, Żychliński's wartime memoirs provide, in addition

---

The master of the ship was John L. Taylor, which agrees with Żychliński's memoirs. Although the date is *after* the date indicated for his enlistment, this may be due to the manifest date being the date of submission rather than the actual date of arrival.

[4]Regimental Descriptive Book, Company E, p. 2, Independent Battalion of Light Infantry [New York] ("Les Enfans Perdu"), Record Group 94, and Regimental Papers, Record Group 94, Box 3429, National Archives, Washington, D.C. A Muster Roll dated July 7, 1862, indicates that he joined the service on April 12 and mustered in on April 14. A Clothing Book for Company E indicates that he received a uniform and enlisted at New York City on April 18. The latter lists his rank as sergeant and his name is signed as "Louis de Zychliński of Guarda." A return for Company B for July, 1862, lists "Louis Zychlinsky," as a private discharged for disability on July 11, 1862. The muster roll for June 30 to August 31, 1862, indicates that he received no pay after June 30 and was "Discharged for disability at Yorktown Va on July 11, 1862." It is possible that his formal discharge was recorded as Yorktown, where his regiment was then encamped, although he may personally have been in New York City at the time. It is possible that personal vanity, of which he has been accused, caused him to assume an aristocratic persona and to embellish his own accomplishments. His demotion to private may indicate that he proved unequal to his boasts, or it may simply be that the lack of a full compliment of soldiers in his company resulted in a corresponding reduction in the number of non-commissioned officers.

[5]*Official Records*, Series I, Vol. 1, Part 3, p. 138, Special Orders #138, dated May 2, 1862, details the *Enfans Perdu* to garrison duty at Gloucester, Virginia, under General James H. Van Alen.

to interesting descriptions of his adventures, reflect the frustration and anger felt by many of McClellan's supporters during the difficult period before the general's removal from command in late 1862.

During his service on the Peninsula, the Pole claimed that his unit was engaged during the Battle of Williamsburg at the beginning of May, 1862, and in several other skirmishes. During one of the latter episodes he describes being injured and invalided out of the service. Indeed, the regimental papers of the *Enfans Perdu*, on file in the National Archives, indicate that Żychliński suffered a rupture during combat on June 18, 1862. As a result, he was sent to Baltimore for treatment, and on July 8 traveled to New York where he was discharged after four months in the Army because his injury left him permanently unfit for service.[6]

Thusfar, the basic outline of Żychliński's service, as described in his 1862 memoir, can be authenticated from existing battalion papers. Yet, in his latter memoirs, published twenty years later in 1882, he maintains that following his discharge in 1862 he traveled to Boston where he resided for some time before again joining the army. The nature of this service remains a mystery. It is possible that he rejoined his original unit, but the records on file in the National Archives are not complete and do not shed further light on his career, if any, in the *Enfans Perdu*. Since he was then residing in Boston, it is possible that he enlisted in a Massachusetts regiment, but a review of the records in the Adjutant General's Office for the Commonwealth of Massachusetts in Boston, and the standard sources for Massachusetts soldiers in the Civil War indicates no evidence that he served in any Bay State regiment.[7]

Żychliński's initial memoir of the American Civil War, *Pamiętniki z wojny amerykańskiej*, bore notation "Boston, November 1, 1862." If we take this as the date he completed or submitted the memoir for publication, then his second service must have occurred between that time and April, 1863, when he claims that he left the United States for Poland to participate in the Polish Uprising. It is possible that he rejoined his original unit and that the fragmentary nature of the surviving

---

[6]See note 4.

[7]Military Records Section, Adjutant General's Office, Military Division, Commonwealth of Massachusetts; *The Massachusetts Soldiers, Sailors and Marines in the Civil War* (Norwood, MA: Norwood Press, 1931, 8 vols.); *Massachusetts in the Army and Navy During the War of 1861-1865* (Boston: Wright & Potter, 1895-96, 2 vols.).

Ludwik Żychliński
From a Contemporary Drawing
[*Courtesy of Eugene Podraza*]

records accounts for the lack of any substantiating evidence in the Regimental Descriptive Books and Regimental Papers. Yet, other possibilities also exist.

In his memoirs, Żychliński maintains that following his recuperation he contacted General Hooker asking to be recalled to the army and subsequently served as a staff officer. Since he had apparently met Hooker during his service in McClellan's Peninsula Campaign, and Hooker still held a prominent position in the Army of the Potomac, it is reasonable that Żychliński would contact Hooker about a recall, especially if he were seeking a staff position or other appointment beyond the rank of common soldier. General Hooker was, in fact, with the Army of the Potomac during the fall of 1862 and was appointed to command of that force following the Battle of Fredericksburg in December, 1863. The Pole's memoirs suggest that this may well have been what occurred. He describes, for example, how, upon hearing of the Polish January Insurrection in 1863 he asked Hooker for a release to leave for Poland. Hooker was at the time busy planning a campaign and would not entertain his release. Żychliński indicates that he then went to "the general commanding the corps" to request release. The description of Hooker "planning a campaign" and the Poles' subsequent appeal to "the general commanding the corp" suggest that at the time in question Hooker was not a corps commander, but rather commanding the army. This would place Żychliński's second enlistment in the winter and spring of 1863, corresponding to when Hooker was planning the campaign that would result in the Battle of Chancellorsville. Further, he indicates that he finally left the army "after a bloody battle in which I took part," leaving for Europe aboard the steamship *Saxony* in May, 1863. Although the time sequence would have been very tight, it is possible that he served during the Chancellorsville campaign and was released immediately after the conclusion of that campaign during the first week of May, 1863.

Another possible indication that this second enlistment was spent with the Army of the Potomac is Żychliński's description of a meeting that he had with the president of the United States. President Lincoln paid an official visit to the Army of the Potomac in October, 1862, following the Antietam Campaign. It is generally believed among Polish American historians that Żychliński's description of his meeting with the president refers to that visit. Military records indicate, however, that his regiment was on duty on the York Peninsula at that time, more than one hundred miles from where Lincoln and McClellan met in northern Virginia. The description here may refer to a visit which Lincoln made to McClellan's troops on the Peninsula earlier that year. On May 4 Lincoln traveled by ship down the Chesapeake, arriving at Fortress Monroe on May 5 and spending several days on the Peninsula. During this visit he was accompanied by Secretary of War Stanton, Secretary of the Treasury Chase, General John E. Wool, Flag Officer Louis M. Goldsborough, and others on an inspection tour of camps about two miles from Fortress Monroe before visiting Norfolk which had only recently been taken from the Confederates. It may have been during this visit to the camps outside Fortress Monroe that the meeting Żychliński describes took place.[8] Lincoln also visited Harrison's Landing on the York Peninsula in July following the Battle of Malvern Hill, but he arrived there on July 8 and by this time Żychliński would have been enroute to Baltimore to recuperate from his injury.

Yet, it is interesting to note that Żychliński never mentioned meeting the president in his first memoir written much more closely to the event than the 1882 publication. In the latter memoir, in the same section as his description of his meeting the president, he notes that he was introduced by General Hooker and that at the same time the Russians were "already slaughtering Poles in Warsaw." This description would fit well with the contention that he served with Hooker's Army of the Potomac in the spring of 1863. In early April of that year, at a time when the January Insurrection was underway in Poland, Lincoln visited Hooker's army for several days during which he conducted reviews of the various corps and met with officers and soldiers. With him were several Cabinet officers and members of Congress, which also fits with Żychliński's description.

A search of the existing records of staff officers does not list Żychliński's name, but once again these records are incomplete and the lack of evidence in this case does not prove that his version is incorrect. It is also possible that he served as a volunteer aide-de-camp, a frequent occurrence during the war. However, in his memoirs he indicates that he had difficulty obtaining a release to return to Poland. If he were a volunteer aide-de-camp he could, of course, leave at any time. If he were a commissioned officer he could legally resign his commission and leave, but would be bound to remain on duty until the resignation was accepted which might account for his delay in leaving. Only as a private or non-commissioned officer would he find it difficult to secure release from the army unless he could obtain a certificate of disability or other such documentation. Thus, it appears that he probably rejoined the army as a private soldier or in a non-commissioned capacity. Perhaps, he may have been promoted to non-commissioned officer rank and may

---

[8]For Lincoln's trips to the Peninsula, see Carl Sandburg, *Abraham Lincoln. The War Years* (New York: Harcourt, Brace & World, Inc., 1967), Vol. 1, pp. 486-487, 495. See also Stephen W. Sears, *To the Gates of Richmond. The Peninsula Campaign* (New York: Ticknor & Fields, 1992), pp. 89-92.

have served at regimental headquarters or in some other capacity which he later elaborated into that of a "staff officer." Regardless of rank, the circumstantial evidence suggests that he did enter the service a second time as he claimed.

Unfortunately, his 1882 memoirs are confusing, and sometimes even contradictory, when describing his second term of service. In it he describes meeting President Lincoln, an encounter with Indians, and many other episodes that he does not mention in his earlier 1862 memoir. We are thus left to conclude that these events took place during his second enlistment. In the current translation, this second memoir begins with Chapter 4 where Żychliński describes army life and indicates that he resigned in April, 1863, to fight in the Polish insurrection. Although some of his descriptions in this memoir appear to indicate that he was serving in the Army of the Potomac under General Hooker, other information tends to support the theory that he rejoined his former battalion.

According to Frederick H. Dyer's *A Compendium of the War of the Rebellion* and the regimental papers of the *Enfans Perdu* on file in the National Archives, Żychliński's unit served in the garrisons at Gloucester Point and Yorktown, Virginia, until December, 1862. Although the regiment did see action at Williamsburg on September 9, it is unlikely that it saw any further action other than guard duty and some routine patrols. In December, 1862, it was assigned to the Department of North Carolina where it served in several siege campaigns in North and South Carolina, seeing action at Morris Island on September 7, 1863, and in the bombardment and siege of several important Confederate cities and strongholds. On January 30, 1864, the remaining troops in the *Enfans Perdu* were consolidated into the 47th New York Volunteer Infantry, which was assigned to the District of Florida in February, 1864. In Florida the regiment took part in an expedition from Jacksonville to Lake City (February 7-22, 1864), participated in the Battle of Olustee (February 20), and was active in the occupation of Palatka (March 10).[9]

Aside from Żychliński's descriptions of events, there are precious few clues that would assist in identifying time and place. In the 1882 publication he describes numerous patrols, reconnaissances and skirmishes which could have taken place either with Hooker's command or

---

[9]Frederick H. Dyer, *A Compendium of the War of the Rebellion* (New York: Thomas Yoseloff, 1959), pp. 191, 199, 299, 694.

with his original battalion on the Yorktown Peninsula.[10] There were numerous patrols and skirmishes in each location. In fact, Żychliński describes an expedition that took place in June, 1863, and included some 500 infantry, 250 cavalry, and four light artillery guns. If he left for Poland in April or May, 1863, as he claims, then clearly the date of June, 1863, must be incorrect. This expedition does, however, correspond closely to a reconnaissance from Yorktown commanded by Gen. Henry M. Naglee which passed through Gloucester, Matthews, King & Queen, and Middlesex Counties. The movement took four days and included a mixed force of troops from four infantry regiments, two squadrons of cavalry and an artillery battery, roughly the same size and duration of time that Żychliński describes.[11]

Yet, a third possibility exists. As indicated above, in December 1862 the *Enfans Perdu* was reassigned to the Department of North Carolina where it participated in several military operations. It is possible that Żychliński's recollections of skirmishes and cavalry patrols dates from service in the Carolinas between December 1862 and April 1863. In fact, many of the circumstances he describes lend themselves very well to the movements of the *Enfans Perdu* during this period.

Although Żychliński asserts that he took part in an expedition toward the Missouri River near St. Louis, he is undoubtedly wrong on this aspect of his service. His descriptions, however, do coincide quite closely with the activities of his old regiment during this period. Two possibilities exist. The first is that Company B, the unit to which he was attached when he was first discharged in July, 1862, and to which he may have returned, was on detached service at Point Lookout, Maryland, in the spring of 1863. It is possible that this movement led Żychliński, whose command of English and American geography were no doubt superficial at best, to believe that he was much farther west than was actually true.[12]

The other, and more likely possibility is that he rejoined the main body of the battalion in the Department of North Carolina. In his 1882 memoir Żychliński indicates that he took part in an expedition under a "General MacDonald." Although a review of William F. Amann's *Personnel of the Civil War*, which lists over 2,500 persons who held either full or brevet ranks of general in the Union Army during the Civil War,

---

[10]Hooker's troops regularly patrolled and skirmished with Confederates during the preparations for the Chancellorsville Campaign, and similar activities took place on the Peninsula.

[11]For Naglee's expedition, see, *Official Records*, Series I, Vol. 18, pp. 49-51.

[12]See the battalion returns in Record Group 94, Box 3428, National Archives; *Official Records*, Series I, Vol. 25, Part 2, p. 5 and Series I, Vol. 18, pp. 532, 574.

fails to uncover the surname MacDonald, there was a Colonel C.R. MacDonald who led the 47th New York Volunteer Infantry, a unit that not only served in the Department of North Carolina but was assigned to the same brigade as the *Enfans Perdu* and was the regiment into which the *Enfans Perdu* were consolidated in January, 1864. It is quite possible that this was the MacDonald to whom Żychliński referred.[13]

In Chapter 4 he alludes to an incident he claims to have personally witnessed "the time that we stood by the sea in the enemy state of Florida." The *Enfans Perdu*, as part of the 47th New York, were transferred to Florida in February, 1864. Further, the reconnaissance that he describes taking part in under the command of "General MacDonald" involved an encounter with Indians who spoke a "broken English and Creole," and a countryside that included "swamps and pristine forests," poisonous snakes, "alligators teeming in the swampy arms of the river," deer, wild turkeys, mosquitoes, the "shrill calls of night birds," and "American lions." Many of these circumstances could indicate a description of his service in the Carolinas prior to May, 1863, and all would fit quite nicely with a description of the deployment of the 47th New York to Florida and its subsequent operations from Jacksonville to Lake City, Olustee and Palatka. The problem with this scenario, of course, is that the Florida expedition took place in the spring of 1864 and Żychliński indicates that he left the United States for Poland in May, 1863, nearly a year earlier. Further, various Polish secondary sources support his contention that he participated in the Polish insurrection as early as July, 1863. Thus, the exact nature of his second enlistment must remain speculative unless, and until, further evidence surfaces.

Regardless of the exact nature of his further service in the Union Army, Żychliński's attention was suddenly diverted from America in the Spring of 1863 when news of the January Uprising in Poland arrived in the United States. To Żychliński, his duty to Poland outweighed any other concerns. Thus, in May of 1863 he boarded the ship *Saxony* for Europe where he hoped to use his military experience to the benefit of his homeland. On arrival he was given the rank of major in charge of the *"Dzieci Warszawy"* [Children of Warsaw] partisan unit operating in the Rawicz and Warsaw districts.[14]

---

[13] William F. Amann, *Personnel of the Civil War* (New York: Thomas Yoseloff, 1961).

[14] *Wielka Encyclopedia*, Vol. 12, p. 870. Żychliński's participation as commander of the "Dzieci Warszawy" unit is confirmed, among others, by Jan Jeziorański, *Zapomniany Bohater 1863 Roku* (London: Katolicki Ośrodek Wydawniczny "Veritas"), p. 40; Stanisław Góra, *Partyzantka na Podlasiu 1863-1864* (Warszawa: Wydawnictwo Ministerstwa Obrony Narodowej, 1976), p. 180-183; and Ryszard Szwed, *Powstanie*

Hindered by a serious lack of arms, the Polish insurgents sacrificed much to smuggle the necessities of war through enemy controlled territory.[15] The habitual lack of adequate resources greatly curtailed the insurgents' ability to engage in large-scale, sustained operations against the enemy. In this atmosphere, Żychliński's command, which sometimes numbered as many as 1,000 troops, fought numerous partisan skirmishes with Russian forces in the vicinity of Warsaw and Podlasie. His first major action, which occurred after his inexperienced soldiers had been in the field only four days, took place when he encountered a force of two and one-half companies of infantry and one hundred Cossacks near the village of Ossa in the Opoczno district, on July 10, 1863. Though new to the rigors of combat, Żychliński's troops forced the enemy from the field inflicting losses of 28 killed and capturing five prisoners including an officer. His own losses included four killed and sixteen wounded, and his report of the engagement noted with pride that his troops fought bravely.[16]

Despite other successes, Żychliński's career in Poland was not an unbroken series of victories. On August 8 he was wounded in action, and soon after his return the Russians dispatched a strong force from Warsaw on August 24 consisting of six companies of infantry, a squadron of lancers and two units of Cossacks numbering 1,200 infantry and 400 uhlans and Cossacks under the command of General Meller-Zakomelski. On the following day this force overtook Żychliński's unit of some 100 riflemen and scythe-bearers and 350 cavalrymen between Żelazna and Wola Starogrodzka. With an approximately four-to-one numerical superiority, the Russians routed Żychliński's troops, forcing the major to seek refuge across the Vistula River. Russian sources claim some 300 of Żychliński's men killed and captured, while Polish sources cite about 46 dead and a large number wounded.[17]

Justyn Sokulski's analysis of Żychliński's activities in Poland suggests that he possessed good organizational talents, a healthy quantity of perseverance, and a loyalty which bound him to his unit in even the most trying of times. Yet, he also exhibited limited intelligence that was easily overshadowed by his obvious vanity and tactless nature, and he

---

Styczniowe w Zagłębiu Dąbrowskim (Warszawa: Państwowe Wydawnictwo Naukowe, 1978), p. 161.

[15]Szwed, *Powstanie Styczniowe*, p. 161.

[16]Góra, *Partyzantka*, p. 180-183; S. Kieniewicz and I. Miller, *Prasa Tajna*.

[17]Góra, *Partyzantka*, p. 180-183; Justyn Sokulski, "The True Face of Ludwik Żychliński," *Historical Contributions*, p. 66.

often showed a darker side which led him to sanction brutality by his troops.[18]

Hampered by the continuing lack of arms and munitions, Żychliński's "Children" fought on through the fall into the increasingly cold winter months until their commander was finally captured by the Russians in December, 1863, and placed on trial. He initially received a death sentence, but a lengthy investigation cited unspecified mitigating circumstances in recommending the reduction of his sentence to twenty years at hard labor. This sentence began on May 22, 1864, when he was sent to the Nerczynsk mines in Siberia.[19] In his memoirs, Benedykt Dymbowski charged that Żychliński avoided the gallows because while in prison he informed on many of his contacts in the Congress Kingdom, thus saving his life but earning for him a reputation as an informant. This explanation, however, should be viewed with caution as Henryk Skok, in his history of the Polish exiles in Siberia, refers to Żychliński as one of the most reliable of the memoirists from that period and explains that while in Darasunie a conflict arose between a him and a faction led by Dymbowski. According to Skok, Żychliński condemned an affair that Dymbowski had with the wife of a shopkeeper from Czyta who came to Darasunie to be treated by Dr. Dymbowski. Because of this, Skok felt that Dymbowski was unduly critical of Żychliński, accusing him of lying in his memoirs and of other transgressions.[20]

In his own memoirs, Żychliński, perhaps in an attempt to prove his innocence of these charges, explained that when saying goodbye to his family at the railroad station in Prague before his journey to Siberia he was accompanied by several Russians including the head of the investigating commission charged with prosecuting those who were active in the rebellion. It was from this innocent association, he claimed, that some suspected the worst. Despite those who judged him harshly, Żychliński asserted that "those who know me, knew that I had a clean conscience because Poland was and is my goal and I never will betray freedom, equality and independence."[21]

---

[18]Sokulski, p. 66.

[19]*Wielka Encyclopedia*, Vol. 12, pp. 870-871; Kieniewicz, et al., *Zarys Powstania Styczniowego*, p. 449; Sokulski, p. 66.

[20]Henryk Skok, *Polacy nad Bajkałem 1863-1883* [The Poles Near Bajkal 1863-1883] (Warsaw: Państwowe Wydawnictwo Naukowe, 1974), p. 131. For Żychliński's comments on Dymbowski, see Ludwik Żychliński, *Przygody Więznia Politycznego* [Adventures of a Political Prisoner] (Poznań: 1884), p. 9.

[21]Ludwik Żychliński, *Pamiętnik byłego dowódcy dzieci warszawsich i b. naczelnika sił zbrojnych powiatów warszawskiego i rawskiego, Ludwika Żychlińskiego* [Memoir of

Though imprisoned and exiled to the brutal Siberian plains, Żychliński nevertheless continued to plot, taking an active part in intrigues among the Poles in Siberia and participating in the Bajkal Uprising in 1865.[22] Dymbowski maintains that in the first camp he was assigned to, Żychliński became involved in a plot against the Czarist authorities and was consequently transferred to another camp in Bajkal, which was deeper in Siberia. There, told the authorities that he was an American citizen and that the American Minister to St. Petersburg would soon intervene to have him freed. When this ruse did not work, Dymbowski maintains that Żychliński stated that he was ready to take an oath not to engaged in conspiracies again. Eventually, his various intrigues led to a transfer to Czyta where, again according to Dymbowski, he was once again accused of betraying fellow Poles, leading to further transfers.[23]

Eventually gaining his release in 1868, he returned to Poland where he settled in Galicia.[24] There, in later years, he penned a series of memoirs that, supplemented by his earlier recollections of the American Civil War, provide both biographical information and a rare glimpse into the mind and perspective of an ardent Polish patriot who viewed all of his experiences, whether in Poland, Italy, America or Siberia, in terms of the values he learned in his youth.

His published reminiscences include *Pamiętniki z wojny amerykańskiej 1862 r.* [Memoir of the American Civil War in 1862 (1863)], *Pamiętniki byłego dowódcy dzieci warszawskich* [Memoir of the Former Leader of the Children of Warsaw (1885)], *Przygody Wielkopolanina w Azji i Ameryce* [The Adventures of a Pole in Asia and America (1882)], *Przygody więźnia politycznego* [The Adventures of a Political Prisoner (1884)], and *Wrażenia i przygody zesłanego w Sybir Wielkopolanina* [Impressions and Adventures of an Exiled Pole in Siberia (1883)].[25]

The Polish patriot died in Bruśno, in the Lubaczów district, in 1891.[26]

---

the Former Leader of the Children of Warsaw, Ludwik Żychliński] (Poznań: 1885), p. 280.

[22]*Wielka Encyclopedia*, Vol. 12, p. 871.

[23]Benedykt Dymbowski, *Pamiętnik dra Benedyta Dybowskiego* (Lwów: 1930), p. 94.

[24]*Wielka Encyclopedia*, Vol. 12, p. 871; Kieniewicz, et al., *Zarys Powstania Styczniowego* , p. 449; Kieniewicz and I. Miller, *Prasa Tajna.*

[25]*Wielka Encyclopedia, Vol. 12, p. 871.*

[26]*Wielka Encyclopedia*, Vol. 12, p. 870; *Encyklopedja Powszechna* indicates that he died in Wrocław.

The Memoirs of Ludwik Żychliński

Reminiscences of the American Civil War,
Siberia, and Poland

Chapter 1

From Poland to America

The hot martial blood that flowed in the veins of the Polish knights who, through many centuries, protected the fatherland from invasions by Germans, Teutonic Knights, Tartars, Turks and other enemies of the Polish state, did not congeal during the difficult and bloody period of national servitude which followed the Partitions.[1] Proof of the continuation of this spirit can be seen in the many occasions on which young Poles, upon hearing that a war for freedom, faith, or independence was raging in some corner of Europe, or even abroad, rushed to stand among the ranks of those fighting for these noble ideas and aspirations, thus experiencing the gallant impressions of the battlefield and thereby

---

[1]Following the weak monarchy of King Augustus III (1734-1763), Poland was split politically between the followers of the Potocki family, who sought the support of France and urged the adoption of an aristocratic constitution, and those who were aligned with the Czartoryski family who sought Russian support and a strengthening of the royal authority. In 1768 the Confederation of Bar was formed as an anti-Russian movement which triggered civil war and a Russian invasion. On August 5, 1772, Russia, in league with Prussia and Austria, carried out the First Partition of Poland, dismembering her borderland areas and dividing these amongst themselves. Later, on May 3, 1791, the Polish diet passed a liberal constitution which resulted in a Second Partition (January 23, 1793) in which additional territories were taken by Russia and Prussia, and the Poles were forced to accept a treaty under which Russia reserved the right to control Poland's foreign relations. Finally, in 1795 a national uprising against Russia and Prussia occurred under the leadership of Tadeusz Kościuszko. The defeat of this rebellion resulted in the Third Partition (October 24, 1795) in which the remaining portions of Poland were completely dismembered and divided between Russia, Prussia and Austria. Despite brief periods of restricted independence for portions of the nation during the time of Napoleon I, Poland remained a subjugated and occupied nation until 1919 when an independent republic was recreated from the ashes of World War I.

learning the art of war.[2] Since his earliest days in the cradle, each was taught that the time would eventually arrive when he would be called upon to willingly and bravely take a stand for the Fatherland. Indeed, throughout the centuries the love of freedom was so deeply rooted in the hearts of Poland's sons that they knew better than most the price of losing freedom and independence.

Following the final partition of Poland, it was feelings such as these which motivated Kościuszko, Pułaski, and other Polish heroes and representatives of freedom who hastened across the ocean to fight for freedom and independence.[3] They richly deserve everlasting memory, glory, and gratitude from the free citizens of the powerful and rich American republic whose foundation the immortal Washington constructed with the assistance of LaFayette, Kościuszko, and Pułaski, who perished at the head of a column during the assault on the entrenchment at Savannah, thus burying with military honors the last standard of thee Confederation of Bar and proving to the free citizens of America that a Pole is always willing to sacrifice his life on the altar of freedom.

It was these principles which led the sons of Poland to the Napoleonic legions.[4] It was not their fault that they were later cheated,

---

[2]The Polish nation has had a long history of assisting others in the defence of their homelands and freedoms. As far back as 1683, King Jan III Sobieski led Polish soldiers to the relief of Vienna when it was besieged by Turkish invaders. During the period of the Partitions, Tadeusz Kościuszko, Kazimierz Pułaski and several other Poles fought for their ideals of freedom in the American Revolution, while many of their countrymen fought under the banners of such movements as the Hungarian Revolt, the Garibaldi movement, or the Paris Commune. Indeed, so widespread was the Polish participation in European revolutionary circles that the Poles adopted an unofficial military motto during this period: "For Your Freedom and Ours."

[3]Kazimierz Pułaski was appointed the first general officer responsible for cavalry operations in the American army during the Revolutionary War. Many historians credit him with saving Washington's army from rout at the Battle of Brandywine, and with advocating changes in the colonial concept of cavalry doctrine which enhanced the effectiveness of that arm of the service. He was mortally wounded while leading an assault upon the British works at Savannah, Georgia, on October 9, 1779.

Tadeusz Kościuszko, one of the first foreigners to offer his services to the Revolution, was appointed colonel of engineers in the Continental Army in 1776, later rising to the rank of brigadier general. He was responsible for designing the river defenses along the Delaware River, fortified the American position at Saratoga leading to one of the decisive battles of the war, and later designed and constructed the fortifications at West Point which today house the United States Military Academy. He later returned to Poland to lead the uprising against the occupying powers in 1794. He died in exile in Switzerland on October 15, 1817.

[4]Tens of thousands of Poles flocked to the colors of Napoleon I in the belief that a French victory over Russia, Prussia and Austria would result in freedom and independence for their native land. The Poles served Napoleon well in virtually all of

abused, exploited and wasted as cannon-fodder for this despot who eventually destroyed the very Revolution which brought him to prominence. This Revolution began with the murder of innocent victims and from the anarchy of such monsters as Marat, Robespierre and other fanatics who believed only in reason and human strength and mocked the laws of God and His commandments.

Poles fought for these same principles of freedom and independence in 1831, on the battlefields of Ksiaz, Mislaw and Września in 1848, in Hungary, in Baden, and finally in Italy in 1859, 1860, and 1861 where their struggles against the Austrians were remembered with honor by Victor Emmanuel. The unselfishness, courage and military prowess of the Poles are known and highly valued, even by the enemies of Poland. Their patriotism is so well known and valued that during the Franco-Prussian war the Prussian generals, whose regiments included many Polish troops from the Poznań territorial Landwehr of East and West Prussia, ordered their bands to play Polish national melodies in the hope of inspiring soldiers who were ordered to fight and die on foreign soil for what were to them incomprehensible, and even repugnant intentions.

The same ideals of freedom brought our hero from the uprising of 1863, Hauke-Bosak,[5] to the ranks of the armies of the French Republic in defense of which he perished on the battlefield. Yet France, thus liberated from attack, did not offer a single sign of gratitude to any son of Poland. But, on the contrary, it humbled itself for its egotistical goals of revenge before the biggest enemy of Poland and freedom, before the absolute Czar of Moscow, seeking assistance in the eternal enemy of freedom for an alliance against Germany.[6] Even after the fall of Napoleon III, this republic, acting from self-interest rather than from principle, withdrew the support that had been granted by the French royal governments to the Poles fighting in defense of France and her freedom. The Poles have a right to this support from the French nation not only because of the blood which they shed in defense of the French standard on numerous battlefields, but also because Napoleon I illegally removed from the Polish treasury at least thirty million francs. Thus,

---

his major campaigns, and units of the Polish army were incorporated into the Emperor's personal bodyguard in honor of their performance and that of their countrymen. A contingent of Poles also followed Napoleon into exile. The Polish national anthem is derived from the marching song of one of the Polish legions which fought with Napoleon in Italy.

[5]Józef Hauke-Bosak served as one of the more prominent military leaders of the Polish revolutionaries during the uprising in 1863.

[6]This is a reference to the fact that Napoleon I, when at the zenith of his power, concluded an alliance with Czarist Russia which fell short of guaranteeing Polish national independence in order to gain other political considerations.

France remains indebted to the Poles for this sum. Furthermore, when Czar Nicholas, calling himself the King of Poland, demanded the repayment of this debt, the French government agreed. Thus France, in return for the blood generously shed by the Poles in her defense and on the island of Santo Domingo,[7] owes aid and hospitality to the Polish exiles. Yet, the present Republic treated our exiles terribly in order to please the Czar and his government. The Commune took revenge on the Third Republic for this ingratitude.[8] Thus, if several individuals of Polish nationality belonged to the Commune, it was the ingratitude which the French in Bordeaux showed to Bosak that forced them to take that step. Besides, Jarosław Dąbrowski,[9] the leader of the Commune, came from the school of the Moscow Czars where he learned communist principles, not from Polish schools where one learns the value of noble martyrdom, the sacrificing of one's self for the defense of freedom and other loftier principles.

By thus reviewing the reasons which led Poles to enlist in foreign ranks, one can refute the charge that they were mere adventurers, of which we are often accused by debased journalists or those who write lies while in the pay of our enemies. At the same time I am providing this background as a means of justifying my reasons for going overseas to fight after the completion of the campaigns in Italy.

Following the liberation of Italy from the Austrian yoke and the consolidation of the Neapolitan Kingdom into one Italian crown, General Cialdini issued the wretched daily order under whose authority the foreign officers who served under Garibaldi, assisting him in the conquest of the Kingdom of the Two Sicilies, were removed from the army and provided with a bonus amounting to one year's pay. Because of this, many Poles left the Italian ranks and went to America where the bloody and murderous Civil War was raging over the question of the abolition

---

[7]Faced with a rebellion of the oppressed peoples in Santo Domingo (today Haiti), Napoleon I sent a number of troops, including 3,000 Poles from the Vistula Legion under General Karol Kniaziewicz, to the island to subdue the insurrectionists. Many Poles fell victim to the tropical fevers rampant on the island, while others, once they determined that their mission was to deny freedom and independence to others, went over to the side of the revolutionaries. It has been estimated that only about 300 of the original number survived the uprisings and diseases.

[8]This is a reference to the Paris Commune movement of 1870 in which many Poles took an interest, one of whom, Jarosław Dąbrowski, was selected as military commander of the Commune's forces.

[9]Jarosław Dąbrowski, a thirty-five year old Polish nobleman and veteran of the 1863 uprising, was chosen military commandant of Paris by the Communards. Generally regarded as one of the Commune's most talented officers, he rapidly raised and trained forces and led them in a valiant stand behind barricades erected to interdict the city's streets.

of slavery. I went with them to further educate myself in this bloody trade because at that time in Poland, and especially among Poles living abroad, thoughts about liberating the homeland from under the yoke of oppression abounded. In them, the Poles generally counted upon the assistance of Napoleon III who desired to establish his own dynasty in France and thus form a balance of power in Europe. That Napoleon III entertained these intentions can be clearly proven through a communication to General Mierosławski[10] from the Central Revolutionary Committee in Europe warning us and hastening our preparations for an uprising in Poland. Polish military schools then opened in order to provide military education to Polish youth. But shameful scenes of discord between Langiewicz,[11] Mierosławski and others discouraged me, and experienced people advised me not to join the camp. Instead, they gave me letters of recommendation to influential persons in the United States where I then went. Much is also said that the Agriculture Society, headed by Andrzej Zamoyski,[12] who is known for his patriotism and his honest way of thinking, had a voluntary plan to make the peasantry into landowners and therefore to unite all townspeople into a general movement whose goal would be the liberation of the subjugated Fatherland. Revolutionary committees in all of Europe sympathized with the Poles in this work and encouraged us to battle against absolutism. They even solemnly promised us moral and material help. Confidential conversations between Napoleon III and Prince Adam Czartoryski[13] clearly gave us the understanding that an uprising in Poland would find support in France, Austria and even in England. We

---

[10]Ludwik Mierosławski (1814-1878) took part in the Polish uprising in 1830-31, and then led the abortive insurrection of 1846. A member of an international revolutionary organization in Europe, he also took part in the uprising in 1848 and the Polish insurrection of 1863.

[11]Marian Langiewicz was one of the more celebrated leaders of the insurrectionary forces during the 1863 uprising, and was a member of the moderate "whites" during the Revolution.

[12]As Chancellor to the Crown and the principal legal advisor to the Czartoryski family, Andrzej Zamoyski was responsible for a number of significant economic and administrative reforms, including the institution of a "Permanent Council" which was not unlike the President's Cabinet developed in the United States, a proposal for a recodification of Polish law, and service on the innovative Commission on Public Education.

[13]Adam Jerzy Czartoryski (1760-1861) was a leader in the November Insurrection who subsequently, during the period of emigration after 1831, directed the political right from its headquarters in the Hôtel Lambert in Paris.

have proof of this in letters written at this time to Vienna. This induced Klaczko,[14] our publicist, to write favorable articles about Austria in various magazines. These letters were proof that Klaczko was the favorite of Minister Beust. Many years later he even became a secret Austrian adviser in the Ministry of Foreign Affairs. But then, political considerations caused Austria to withdraw from the league of the three emperors and to draw closer to France. I heard all about this from influential people before my departure to America, and even aboard ship the passengers discussed rather loudly the trickery of Napoleon III, whom they disdained and considered a tawny owl of a monarch to whom flock small and great in order to view him up close.

Here I have mentioned very briefly the events in Europe before beginning a description of my adventures in the United States so that the reader can understand the circumstances under which I journeyed to the United States to learn the practical trade of war, and not as a mere adventurer for personal goals and aspirations.

* * * * *

Realizing in January, 1862, that I could not be of any use to my Fatherland sitting in England, and for reasons involving my own entangled affairs, I left London, with the help of my family, on February 1, 1862, on the three-masted schooner *Hemisphere* bound for New York.[15]

The foul northwesterly wind kept us in the channel, first close to the English shore and then to the French shore. For two full weeks we sailed around in the channel until finally, at sunrise on the morning of February 16, the wind changed from east to west and fortunately for us filled our sails.

On February 18 we sailed out of the channel into the Atlantic Ocean, and on the following night I was awakened by a storm of hurricane strength. Having dressed as quickly as possible, but with difficulty because of the extreme rocking of the ship, I went on deck where I was immediately greeted with a bath from a large wave. Although the ship was quite tall, that did not prevent the deck from being washed by the force of the waves. In the extreme darkness I could neither recognize the main mast, nor find a place to support myself. By accident, and

---

[14]Julian Klaczko (1825-1906) was a literary critic, historian and publicist who worked closely with Adam Czartoryski's Hotel Lambert group. In 1870 he served as a representative to the Austrian Council of State.

[15]Records dated April 17, 1862, from the Port of New York on file in the Passenger Ship collections at the National Archives verify Zychliński's arrival aboard the ship *Hemisphere*.

through the desire to save myself, I grabbed a rope which led me to the middle mast. There I recognized the captain who was issuing commands in his loud resonant voice. The feeling which I experienced in the first moment after taking that unexpected bath will never leave my memory. Seeing myself in a secure place, I shook myself and wiped the water from my eyes. I then recognized that there was no danger and called out to ask the captain if I could in some way be of assistance. It seems that my presence amazed the captain who, grabbing me, laughed heartily when he saw that I had taken what he called Neptune's baptism. The storm continued for forty-eight hours and the captain himself admitted that it had been a long time since he had such a greeting. The main mast cracked and we had to reinforce it with poles, chains, and ropes so that it would at least be able to hold the weight of the two mainsails when they were filled with wind.

I was often a witness to storms on both the Baltic and Mediterranean Seas, but I had never seen such a storm or experienced such a feeling. I never saw such a roaring sea and waves so high as I did on this occasion. Some came to extreme heights and many times I saw myself two hundred feet above sea level or in unfathomable depths surrounded with mountains of raging water. This was such a wild and magnificent view that I unintentionally had to thank the Creator of the world and to offer a short and honest prayer to Him who gave nature this magnificent and amazing spectacle.

Finally the storm stopped, the sky cleared up, the waves began to roll more slowly and fair winds drove us with the speed of a shot toward the new world. For six days the winds successfully served us, and I often saw the masts and sails of other ships sailing and swaying majestically through the large ocean. Captain Taylor[16] explained to me the navigational calculations and, although he was an American, he did what he could to make such a monotonous trip a pleasant one for me.

On the morning of February 27 there appeared signs of an approaching storm, but on this occasion we had time to make preparations and we waited quietly. Around noon nature's battle with man began again, a battle of waves against a ship directed with one hand by a man standing at her stern. The captain did what he could to keep the damaged mast up and steered just enough so that the ship could maintain its east to west heading. After a thirty-five-hour battle, the storm had driven us eight hundred nautical miles north of our intended course.

I felt a change in climate and with amazement I found out that we were in the vicinity of icebergs flowing from north to west. When the

---

[16]The passenger manifest of the *Hemisphere* on file in the National Archives lists John L. Taylor as the ship's master.

first rays of the sun appeared, the captain calculated where we were and took a southwesterly course. We sailed in this direction quite peacefully, although constantly through a rough sea, having a wind at our back all the time. On the morning of March 8 I spotted an iceberg while we were near Newfoundland. This is a most dangerous place because of the reefs and shoals that lie hidden beneath the surface of the water.

The captain pointed at the icebergs and said that a thousand ships had sunk in this place because if a ship meets a storm in this area it cannot be saved. Only a miracle could pull it out from between the ice and shoals. Uncontrolable shivers went through me as I looked at our repaired mast and at the strange clouds that had been appearing on the horizon for the last several minutes. I instinctively asked the captain if he expected a storm. He very calmly answered that we would most certainly encounter a storm later that night, and then issued the deck hands the proper orders. I admit that the captain's prediction made an unpleasant impression on me, but being a Pole I did not want to show fear, especially since through the whole month since our sailing I was considered very courageous.

As the captain predicted, that night the storm began with a roar, rushing wind, and indescribable darkness. At first it sounded in the distance, but it eventually came over our heads. The activity was immeasurable among the deck hands, even the captain himself worked. I assisted where I could, hoping that in my work I would forget the danger that threatened us. We spent the whole night working and in the morning the storm subsided a little. I asked the captain if there was still any more danger, but he laughed, answering that there was always danger but that during the night we did not hit any shoals or reefs and now we were not in any immediate danger. He thought that the storm and wind had driven us to the other side of Newfoundland and therefore we avoided the reefs and shoals.

I sighed deeply and with childlike delight took off my wet clothes and threw myself on an uncomfortable bed made of boards. I slept soundly for twenty hours and did not hear them when they tried to awaken me for breakfast or dinner. It was a day later before I again sat at the table with the captain, who greeted me sincerely and joked with me.

After five weeks of sailing the ocean, on the morning of March 9 I saw from the mast the land which the captain had promised, and with a shout of joy I greeted the new world where people seek happiness and

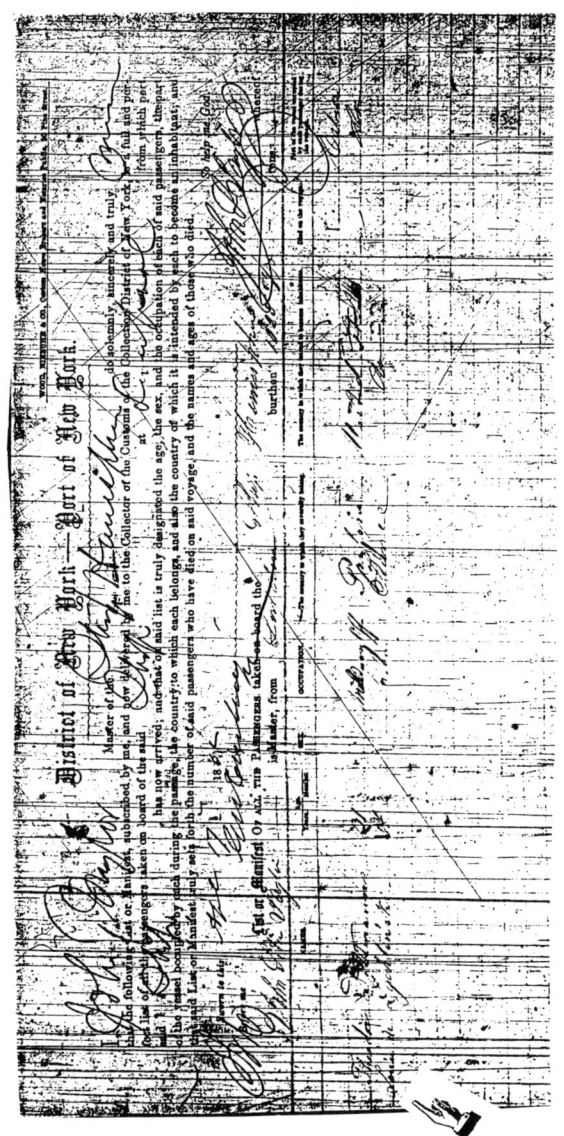

Żychliński's name appears on the manifest of the ship *Hemisphere*
[*Courtesy of the National Archives*]

fortune. On March 10 we stood in the port of New York[17] and after quite a long inspection by the police, doctor, and customs officials, I at last lowered myself on the barge that took me to town amongst the shouting and business of New York.

I will not describe what kind of impression this city made on me, since a similar impression was experienced by every Pole entering a village or trading town in the old or new world. Not having the financial means to tour the town, or time to seek employment and work in New York, I looked only for the hotel that the captain of the ship recommended to me. I wanted to find out where I had to go to see if I could immediately find a place in the army.

---

[17]The passenger manifest of the ship *Hemisphere* is dated April 17, 1862. That may, however, have been the date of submission rather than the actual date of arrival.

Chapter 2

A War Fought for Pay,
Not for Patriotism

In the United States, the Polish soldier is viewed with respect, and his services are willingly and confidently accepted because of the great feeling of gratitude to Kościuszko and Pułaski which is deeply rooted in the hearts of the free citizens of the American republic. Poles are considered to be heroes and champions of freedom, and because of this attitude they are valued and respected even among government circles. Knowing this, and not expecting a new Polish uprising to begin very soon, I sought to obtain practical experience on the battlefields of the New World before the Civil War should end.

When I first inquired, I was told that it was difficult to find a place since there was only one regiment of volunteers being formed in New York and an order had been issued prohibiting the formation of any more. Thus, with letters of recommendation from Paris and London, I went to see Colonel Felix Confort,[1] a Frenchman, who was forming a regiment under the name "*les Enfans Perdu*,"[2] which was comprised primarily of Frenchmen and Germans.

---

[1]Count Felix Confort was a French officer who led the "Enfans Perdu" until his resignation from the service in May, 1863. For sketchy details of his service see Ella Lonn, *Foreigners in the Union Army and Navy* (Baton Rouge: Louisiana State University Press, 1951) and Frederick Phisterer, *New York in the War of the Rebellion 1861-1865* (Albany: Lyon Company, 1912, 5 vols), p. 4118.

[2]The Independent Battalion of Infantry, known as "*Les Enfans Perdu*," was organized at New York City with Companies A through G mustering into service on April 18, 1862. Comprised of immigrant stock of various nationalities, the battalion served

Mr. Confort received me quite coldly and, after reading my letters and talking with me briefly, he told me that he could not give me an officer's position since they were all occupied. However, he indicated that he would be willing to accept me into the ranks of his color guard as a non-commissioned officer. I willingly agreed to his offer and that same day I swore allegiance to the United States of America.[3]

Three days after my induction as a volunteer I was in uniform and left New York for Washington, D.C., with the whole regiment. There, on March 28, we were issued arms and sent directly to the battlefield near Yorktown, in southeastern Virginia, where General McClellan was besieging the Yorktown fortifications securely defended by three divisions of the Confederate Army. But, before I begin to describe the methods by which the armies were formed and the tactics used to fight the battles, I must first describe the organization of the army and the methods used to form regiments and companies.

To recruit soldiers, the President of the United States requests the governors of the various states to form regiments, and the Secretary of War allocates the total number of soldiers required according to the population of the various states and territories. The governor of each state must then supply a certain number of volunteers to the government in Washington in order to form regiments. To do this, the governor grants permission to any lawyer or businessman to form a regiment and to nominate a colonel who then provides a certain sum to assist in the cost of recruiting. The lieutenant colonel, in turn, may agree to provide 100 or 150 men, in this way obtaining the right to appoint the major and the captains. To receive a nomination as captain, one must supply 75 men or the appropriate sum for the cost of their recruiting. The captain must then find a first lieutenant and a second lieutenant. The first lieutenant gives the captain $400, or supplies 40 people. The second lieutenant must give the captain 20 people, or $200 dollars for the cost of recruiting, if he wants to receive an appointment. In this way each offi-

---

with the Fourth Army Corps during McClellan's Peninsula Campaign in the summer of 1862. The battalion was later transferred to the Carolinas where, on January 30, 1864, the unit ceased to exist and the surviving members were transferred to the 47th New York Infantry. For general information on the unit's history see Frederick H. Dyer, *A Compendium of the War of the Rebellion* (Dayton, OH: Morningside, 1979, 3 vols.), pp. 199, 299, 354, 355, 365-369, 1471; Phisterer, pp. 4114-4122.

[3]The Company E Descriptive Book for the *Enfans Perdu* indicates that Żychliński was enrolled as "Louis de Zychlinski" by Captain François Boucher on April 18, 1862. Żychliński was then 5th Sergeant in Company E, but transfered to Company B as Sergeant on April 26 of the same year. He is described as age 27, 5'8", light complexion, grey eyes, brown hair, born in Poland, with an occupation of soldier. He enlisted for three years or the duration of the war. The unit descriptive books and papers of the *Enfans Perdu* are located in the National Archives, Record Group 94.

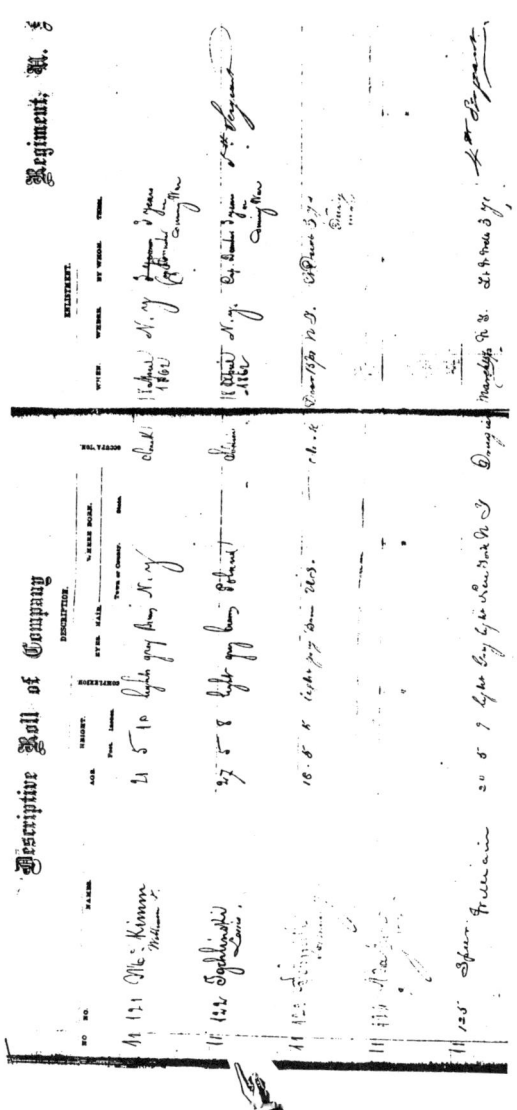

Page from Regimental Returns showing Żychliński as a Sergeant
[*Courtesy of the National Archives*]

cer recruits people for himself and his company. Each officer has his own recruiting office and, once he has a sufficient number of volunteers, requests the rank of colonel. From the moment he swears allegiance to the United States each soldier is paid by the central government and not by the state from which he was recruited. For this reason officers go to taprooms and saloons, and visit newly arrived ships in attempts to induce men to enlist through the use of promises. They intoxicate the simple man in order to get his signature, and then stand him before a commission where he swears loyalty to the central government for three years or the duration of the war.[4]

These soldiers are called "volunteers." They dress, feed, and house them in barracks, or in tents out in the field, until the whole regiment is formed. Once the colonel assembles 1,000 people—that is, ten companies—he receives orders to go to Washington. The regiment is then placed on a steamboat or a train. In Washington they issue the regiment arms and a number, direct it to its assigned division, and then send it straight to the battlefield.

The regiment is usually formed in a period of five or sometimes six months. During the formation of the regiment, the soldiers are trained very little, but are given good food and clothes in order not to discourage other potential recruits. However, this suddenly changes when the regiment is formed and sent into the field where, using the methods of the Muscovites, they teach the soldiers how to maneuver and to work in concert with artillery on the battlefield.

Such means of recruiting and of gathering volunteers have to be condemned by Poles for several reasons. First, the officers themselves are people without military knowledge. Any person can become a major or captain or even a colonel if he has the money for the initial recruiting and knowledge of the place where he is recruiting. It often happens that any shoemaker, merchant or tailor is an officer, while in the ranks may be found educated young men or foreigners who arrive in the country with military knowledge from Germany or France in hope of becoming an officer.[5]

Second, the colonel is usually a merchant who does not have any military knowledge and, like all other officers in the regiment, considers the forming of the regiment as an investment. The monthly pay is as

---

[4]Żychliński is substantially correct about the methods used to recruit Union Army regiments during the Civil War. In fact, the lack of adequate replacement programs and the assignment of officers for political or other reasons, without regard to their prior military service, continued to be a problem which plagued the efficiency and stability of the Northern forces—particularly in the Eastern campaigns—throughout the war.

[5]While there is much truth in Żychliński's account, this sentence certainly betrays his resentment and disgust at not being offered a commission.

follows: colonel, $250; lieutenant colonel, $190; major, $180; captain, $145; first lieutenant, $125; and second lieutenant, $109. The highest non-commissioned officer receives $22, the second highest $20, the third highest $17, and the volunteer $13.

The war is thus fought for pay, not for patriotism, nor for the abolition of slavery.[6] The money is supposed to be paid to the volunteers every two months, but it often happens that they are not paid for as long as eight months. After the war, soldiers have a right either to a $100 bonus or to an equivalent in unsettled land on the plains. Officers only receive their pay every three months, and if they become wounded they have a right to a pension according to their rank. The soldier also has a right to a pension if he is completely incapable of working. In such case, he will receive eight dollars per month for the rest of his life. The pension, however, begins only after the end of the war. As a result, many thousands of wounded soldiers and invalids wander through the streets and roads and die of hunger, unable to begin collecting their pensions until the conclusion of the war.

The military organization and administration are terrible. Both are in the hands of speculators and businessmen, not people with a heart full of love for the fatherland. There are many faults to point out and criticize, but I will not pass judgment on these faults here. I will return to my main intention of describing my stay and observations of the conduct of the present murderous and entangled war.

I briefly described the means of forming volunteer regiments because I think that in Europe, and especially in Poland, no one would understand this *legerdemain*, and would expect, judging by the feelings of a Polish heart, that volunteer units are formed out of patriotism and that such regiments are made up of Americans who love their country and wish to defend their laws and freedoms. By reading newspapers and judging from their descriptions, everyone who thinks or supposes this is mistaken.

---

[6]In this statement Żychliński stretches the truth. At the beginning of the war the lure of patriotism was a very important factor in filling the ranks of both the Northern and Southern armies. In some Northern circles the abolition of slavery was a factor, but it was certainly secondary to patriotism and the desire to preserve the Union. In fact, when President Lincoln issued his first calls for volunteers, so many men turned out that many had to be refused because the government lacked the uniforms and weapons necessary to equip them all. By 1862, when Żychliński entered the service, much of the patriotic lure had evaporated with the lengthening casualty lists. Consequently, though overstating his point, it was true that the government was experiencing increasing difficulty in enlisting new recruits. This led to increasing financial bounties for voluntary enlistments and, in 1863, to a national conscription law.

The army is made up mostly of foreigners; mainly Irishmen, Germans, and various other nationalities.[7] As proof of what I write one need only note that now that there is a shortage of foreigners who, living in poverty, grasp at this last chance and voluntarily choose to enlist in the army, the government must turn to threats of a draft as they do in Prussia or France in order to obtain the required number of soldiers. Native-born Americans who fear becoming soldiers often form committees and promise to pay $100 to anyone who would voluntarily enlist in the army in their place. But even this sum did not attract enough volunteers, consequently they raised the sum to $200 upon enlistment and $100 after the war. Yet, even with that sum they still did not find the quantity required by the government in Washington. Thus, they must assemble men with their own militia and those who are to become soldiers must pull lots. In this way the Americans seek to protect themselves from having to fight for their Constitution and the preservation of the Union. Such behavior proves that Americans do not shed their blood, but only that of the immigrants.[8] The government itself betrayed these politics; as proof of this I draw attention to a proclamation announced by the Secretary of State, which I read in the French and German newspapers, encouraging emigration and offering shelter and employment to the poor Germans and Frenchmen in Europe. This proclamation convinced Europe that the Americans were short of victims and must seek such people in Europe by publicly encouraging emigration through the announcement of this proclamation.[9] This, clearly, explains the political policy of the United States toward European emigration.

---

[7]Soon after the conclusion of the Civil War, Benjamin A. Gould conducted an inquiry into the backgrounds of soldiers. He published his findings under the title *Investigations in the Statistics of American Soldiers* (New York: Riverside Press, 1869). Gould found that nearly 25% of all federal troops were born in foreign countries. Another researcher, Wilhelm Kaufmann, who concentrated only on Germanic immigrants, found that by adding second generation Germans to the original immigrants, the total number of actual Germanic soldiers in uniform in the North represented 37% of the Union Army. His calculations appear in Frederick F. Schrader's *1683-1920* (New York: Concord Publishing Company, 1920).

[8]Żychliński's criticism of Northern patriotism cannot be dismissed as ethnocentrism. Although patriotic feelings were certainly high at the beginning of the war, widespread resistance developed in both the North and South once the draft laws were enacted. The most famous of these were the draft riots in New York City in 1863 which necessitated the withdrawal of Northern troops from the Gettysburg Campaign to quell the disturbances.

[9]Żychliński is quite correct in his assertion that the Northern states attempted to recruit soldiers in Europe. An example on the state level occurred in Massachusetts where 907 Germans were imported to serve as substitutes for Massachusetts natives.

The native-born American in the North hates war and does not have in himself any military courage since all his attention is put in business speculation and he will only fight for money.

The highest offices are reserved for Americans, but the lower officers and soldiers are generally foreigners—those who emigrated from Europe and were not born in America.

Conditions are different in the Southern portion of America, which is called the Confederate States.[10] The Southern states are fighting for their independence from the North. There the personal hatred against the North, and the fear of losing their possessions, brings every single citizen to arms. In the ranks fight the sons of large landowners and citizens of Southern states where each man is a soldier. Wives drive out their husbands, mothers send their sons, in order to repel the Northern invasion and defend their land.[11]

The Northern states are more numerous since they are made up of 21,000,000 people and the Southern states have only 8,000,000 white people and 4,000,000 black slaves. The North is richer in production and food, has a significant fleet that is now equal to that of France, and has a large, organized army, but it will never suppress the South. Proof of this is that to this day, in every battle, the North loses thousands of soldiers, and the armies of the United States are standing in the same place where they were at the beginning of the war.[12]

---

[10]During the course of the war, as volunteer enlistments began to ebb, the Northern government attempted to encourage volunteering by the creation of bonuses which were paid to the soldier upon enlistment. When this proved only partially successful, the government enacted a military draft which was fraught with exemptions for politicians, government workers, and others. It also included provisions that enabled a draftee to purchase an exemption, or to provide a substitute. Contrary to Żychliński's assertion the Confederacy also adopted these same methods, resorting to conscription before the North and including in their list of exemptions a special exemption for one male on each plantation. Neither system was over-endowed with either fairness or equity.

[11]The assertion that commissions in the Southern Army rested less on privilege and political connections is true to only a small extent. The son of Robert E. Lee, the famous Confederate general, served as a private in an artillery battery, but there were many who owed their commissions to position or influence. With regard to Southern enthusiasm for the war effort, statistics show that the desertion rate in the Southern armies remained higher than that in the Union armies throughout the war.

[12]Żychliński wrote this at the end of 1862, after the Northern disasters at First Bull Run, Second Bull Run, in the Peninsula Campaign and the Valley Campaign, and at Fredericksburg. Antietam, the only Northern victory, was not perceived as such by many in view of the enormous casualties. Thus, the general feeling in the North at that time was one of dispair, with many people beginning to harbor anti-war sentiments. Thus, the passage reflects Żychliński's experiences in the Northern defeat on the Peninsula which was fresh in his mind at the time he wrote.

Now I will return to my regiment's trip from Washington to York-town, and to the main events that I witnessed.

Chapter 3

General McClellan's Peninsula Campaign

On March 28, 1862, my regiment, following an inspection and a parade before the President, received an order to go to a waiting steamboat which then sailed for twenty-seven hours and landed us close to the field of battle near Yorktown, Virginia.[1] On the early evening of March 30, we disembarked about three miles from the Yorktown fortress, an important strategic point standing astride the route to the Confederate capital in Richmond. All of this time we were within hearing of the enemy's artillery which fired shells at the besieging soldiers.[2]

The lands around Yorktown, on the side where we landed, are muddy and highly unsuitable for marching, much less constructing a battery to bombard the enemy's fortress. That same night my regiment moved immediately into the battle line where we spent an entire sleepless night by the light of the bursting bombs and shells. Two large mortars made a particular impression with their huge 300-pound bombs which made a terrible sound and shook the ground around us. I com-

---

[1] In March, 1862, General George B. McClellan led the Army of the Potomac south via Chesapeake Bay to the York Peninsula to begin what became known as the "Peninsula Campaign." Landing some 120,000 troops in the vicinity of Yorktown, he planned to move overland in the hope of capturing the Confederate capital at Richmond. Despite Żychliński's later description, historians generally agree that McClellan moved too slowly, often being held up by Confederate forces which he outnumbered by margins of nearly six to one early in the campaign.

[2] Żychliński's dates appear to be in error. The official records indicate that his battalion did not leave New York State until April, 1862; not March as he states. The official dates would also be in accord with the dates of his arrival in the United States.

manded our outpost guard. The next morning rain began to fall and I could see very little of the siege line. I only remember that the canon fire stopped somewhat and I was relieved from my post by a cavalry unit on May 1.

My regiment was eloquently uniformed and made a good impression. We had blue pants, white spats, half boots, a blue overcoat with gold embroidery in the fashion of the French riflemen, a black French cap bordered with gold strings and pinned to the hat was a black feather which fell over our eyes.

Our regiment set up camp as best it could in the muddy forest on the left wing of the siege line, about two English miles from the enemy's battery and in the vicinity of the headquarters of General McClellan. So close did we stand to the enemy that while preparing dinner and coffee I saw our artillery dueling with field guns, in the manner of Napoleon III, with the fortress artillery of the enemy, and I often heard the sound and ping of the bullets flying over the heads of the encamped regiment.

It is necessary to mention that, as it is with all other regiments here, our regiment was not trained and the soldiers comprising it are also not regularly trained and only have a superficial knowledge of the basic movements and manoeuvres. Looking at the proud but frightened soldiers I wondered to myself what they would do if they received an order to go under fire. There were even those who did not know how to use a bayonet, or even understand the commands of our colonel who, though honest, did not know a word of English and could not converse with the Germans and Irishmen who made up half of our regiment.[3]

For several days we did not receive an order and we only trained the soldiers in the use of arms, basic maneuvers, and also taught the soldiers the alphabet. Through all this time the cannon fire did not stop and, although we were in the rear of the battle line, out of sight of the fortress and only hearing the roar of its' cannons, we nevertheless lost three people killed and five wounded when a bomb fell into our camp. For quite a long time we performed our duty by the headquarters and I often had the pleasure of talking with the Comte de Paris and Prince

---

[3]The language barrier was a common problem in Civil War armies, many of which relied on recruiting in ethnic communities or among incoming immigrants. There are several documented cases where, under the stress of combat, officers forgot their limited command of English and began shouting orders in German, French, or some other language. In his autobiography, General McClellan, who was fluent in several languages, relates an incident that took place when he encountered a guard while returning to camp from Washington. "In reply to their challenges," he recounted, "I tried English, French, Spanish, Italian, German, Indian, a little Russian and Turkish; all in vain, for nothing at my disposal made the slightest impression upon them, and I inferred that they were perhaps Gipsies or Esquimaux or Chinese." See *McClellan's Own Story* (New York: Charles L. Webster, 1887), pp. 142-143.

Reuss who served as captains under General McClellan. Several times I saw the general himself visiting our colonel, Felix Confort, who had already made General McClellan's acquaintance in the Crimea and had used the general's support in securing his colonelcy.[4] Since at one time I had the duty of being in command of the honor guard of the general staff, I even had the pleasure of being introduced to the general himself who, knowing that I was a Pole, praised our nation, stating that we Poles are soldiers from childhood and that in our blood lies courage and subordination.

Several days after my arrival I was assigned to the brigade of General Van Alen who was previously a lawyer and had no real knowledge about leading his brigade in an attack since there were no experienced European officers at hand.[5] On May 3, we received the order to break camp and go to the right wing of the battle line where we had to perform police duties [provost guard] whose job it was to arrest deserters and guard the ammunition and the wagons. We did this duty for four days, constantly training in our movements and the use of our arms. On the fifth day our reconnaissance had quite a bloody skirmish with the enemy and we certainly would have been attacked by two enemy divisions if the following event had not occurred. The [Confederate] general commanding Yorktown received an order from Richmond to retreat and leave Yorktown. He thus gave an order to the left wing of the enemy's army to break camp immediately and at night to withdraw to Williamsburg.

At night we heard strong and incessant canon fire on our left wing and in the morning we received an order to attack the enemy at all points. Our wing moved forward to the left wing of the enemy, but we were amazed to find in the forest surrounding us that all of the enemy camps were abandoned. All that we saw after our arrival was a regiment of cavalry and an enemy horse battery withdrawing to the hill behind the forest.

A report given to General McClellan changed our movement and the whole army, consisting of 107,000 soldiers, received an order to advance from Yorktown, in line of battle, toward the position to which the enemy was withdrawing near the outskirts of Richmond, a distance of some eighty-two miles. Thus, our right wing attacked the closest wing of the enemy as it was retreating to the town of Williamsburg, and the center and left wings operated toward Yorktown. Having found the fort

---

[4]McClellan had been an American observer during the Crimean War.

[5]General James H. Van Alen, the son of a wealthy New York merchant, organized and outfitted the 3rd New York Cavalry at his own expense. During the Peninsula Campaign he was placed in command of the posts at Yorktown and Gloucester. He resigned his commission in July, 1863, and returned to civilian life.

and town abandoned they went through the town chasing the retreating enemy along the bank of the York River toward White House on the most convenient road to the capital city of the Confederate States— Richmond. My regiment, being on the right wing of the reserve, did not have a chance to march through Yorktown where the enemy put up a resistance and a battle began. This day in history was called the Battle of Williamsburg. The enemy put up a resistance on the right wing and with this insured the escape of his center wing which retreated as quickly as possible toward the banks of the York River, the shortest road to Richmond.

The Battle of Williamsburg began, as battles usually do here, with an artillery duel.[6] After a four-hour cannonade, the enemy opened with rifle fire and began to drive us from the hills where our artillery operated. At some points our regiment suffered severely. The enemy, with his usual courage, forced us toward our center and threatened us with an attack on our flanks, especially the brigade where my regiment was. The reserve of our right wing attacked together with my regiment. I must admit that although the soldiers were untrained they held their place through two hours of artillery and rifle fire.

---

[6]The Battle of Williamsburg, one of the opening engagements in the Peninsula Campaign, was fought on May 4-5, 1862. It began as a clash between the Confederate rear guard which was covering the withdrawal of Southern forces, and the forward elements of General McClellan's advance. Eventually, some 41,000 federal troops were engaged against 32,000 Confederates. Northern losses were 2,239 compared with 1,603 Southern casualties. The fortifications to which Żychliński alludes were probably the emplacements of Fort Magruder which became a focal point for the federal assaults. Żychliński's role in the battle is problematical. Dyer indicates that his battalion was attached to the 4th Corps without assignment to a specific brigade, but that it served in garrison duty at Gloucester and Yorktown and was not actively engaged in the Peninsula campaign. Phisterer confirms this, and both sources indicate that the Battle of Williamsburg which was fought on September 9, 1862, was its first engagement. Stephen W. Sears' comprehensive study *To the Gates of Richmond: The Peninsula Campaign* (New York: Ticknor & Fields, 1992) does not list the battalion among those units that participated in the campaign. Although not officially part of the army engaged on the Peninsula, as an unassigned regiment in the 4th Corps it is entirely possible that the battalion was indeed called into action from its "official" garrison assignment, especially in view of McClellan's continuous appeals for reinforcement and the fact that it was officially assigned to the 4th Corps which did participate in the campaign. Sears indicates that McClellan and the Comte de Paris did arrive on the battlefield, although late in the day, and raised the spirits of the troops as Żychliński indicates. General Van Alen commanded the posts at Gloucester and Yorktown, and was therefore Żychliński's commanding officer. Thus, it is natural that his "brigade" should be mentioned as coming to the support of the battalion, but it is, however, difficult from the existing narratives and archival materials to determine where the *Enfans Perdu* may have been during the time in question.

General James H. Van Alen
[*Courtesy of the U. S. Military History Institute*]

Our officers lost their heads and hid behind trees and in holes so that during the battle I could not see half of them. Many times I thought that one or the other was wounded or had been killed. However, after the battle, many men appeared, even Captain Hiszpan from my own company who complained that he was felled by a tree shattered by an artillery shell. After holding our position for quite a long time, during which we formed somewhat of a defensive line, our regiment was relieved by the whole brigade of General Van Alen. The main concern then was to hold the grove of trees where my regiment initially took position.

The enemy concentrated two batteries on us in the grove of trees, and then began to scorch us with grape shot, shells, and shrapnel. I thought that this was "The Day of Reckoning" since not only did bullets fall like hail, but trees and branches broken by shots, bomb fragments, and shells fell on my head and wounded our frightened soldiers.

The whole brigade came to help us and then shortly it packed up and began to withdraw in complete disarray to the right of the trees where we stood previously, answering with fire from our platoons the enemy's regiment standing opposite us. General McClellan himself came and raised our spirits. He then ordered us to advance and with our bayonets to disperse the enemy's artillery which was so murderously pounding us. But he himself could not hold his position and left the forest leaving with us the Comte de Paris and Prince Reuss from his staff who encouraged the soldiers as well as they could to keep going and form columns. The enemy attacked us and such anarchy arose on our battle line that I saw officers and soldiers escaping from several regiments by forcing their way through thickets in various directions. I do not know what would have happened to the whole brigade of General Van Alen if our regiment, *Les Enfans Perdu*, and four artillery pieces that held their position, had not prevented the enemy from taking all of us prisoners. During this attack, the Comte de Paris particularly distinguished himself with bravery and quick thinking. We withdrew from the thickets and I admit now that I truthfully and sincerely sighed with relief at seeing myself in an open field and not hearing over my head the breaking of branches and the exploding of shells, bombs and falling shrapnel.

This dogged battle continued on all points, and everywhere the enemy pushed and shot at us. Fortunately our center, which had marched through Yorktown, brought us help and as a result we began to take heart and the enemy began to retreat on the road to Richmond; constantly, however, attacking us with his artillery and cavalry.

The night came and with it the battle ceased. We lost 2,170 dead and 4,837 wounded. The enemy also had to take a significant amount of losses, but without doubt less since he occupied a mountainous and more advantageous position. This was our regiment's baptism and because of the inexperience of the generals and commanding officers, my regiment itself lost 108 killed and 189 wounded.[7]

Today, describing this event, I myself am amazed that my regiment came out of the crossfire in which it found itself for three hours with only these losses, and only to Providence and the grace of God do I ascribe the miracle that I fortunately came out of such a burning hell.

I slept well that night and only in the morning did we bury the dead and look for the wounded. The burying of the dead takes place with the usual military honors, like everywhere in civilized countries. Throughout the whole night our artillery and cavalry slowly advanced toward the retreating enemy and occasionally we heard canon fire or rifle shots from our or the enemy's outposts on our left flank.

On the morning after the Battle of Williamsburg, rain began to fall so heavily and incessantly that we could not make a fire for cooking. Without breakfast and with only biscuits in our knapsacks, we marched constantly toward Richmond behind the enemy who changed direction and withdrew more to the left. Our left wing met with the enemy and again the whole battle line had to stop as the enemy threatened to cut us off. Our left wing began to withdraw toward the center and the enemy pushed constantly, attacking toward our left wing. This maneuver was so well calculated by the enemy that it completely halted our hot pursuit of the retreating army. General McClellan, however, threatened the enemy with the arrival near the walls of the town of Richmond of the right wing under his command. Because of the enemy's constant maneuvering on the left wing, we constantly found ourselves in brush fires and in constant marches. Every day bloody skirmishes took place between the two advanced guards. It seems strange that although we outnumber the enemy, it was not we, but the enemy that attacked and in this way thwarted our pursuit. He always chose an advantageous position and made his stand. From these movements I could judge and gather that we had opposing us good generals and in all from what I saw that the enemy has more capable, better, and braver officers.

We lost four days of time with these constant brushfires. The enemy, being so much weaker than we in regard to the number of infantry, withdrew in an orderly fashion. The enemy's artillery formed a battery to block our road whenever it could find an advantageous posi-

---

[7]Sears lists casualty figures for the Battle of Williamsburg as: Union, 2,283; Confederate 1,682.   Żychliński vastly overstates the losses of his own regiment which totaled only nine enlisted men killed or mortally wounded and fifty-two enlisted men dying of disease *during the entire war.*   Perhaps he may be referring to casulaties suffered by Van Alen's brigade rather than his regiment specifically.

tion for this maneuver. I am certain that through eight days I constantly heard a cannon on various points of the battle line. The soldiers were so weary and weak from the constant marches that General McClellan was forced to hold back the chase and change the position on the whole battle line.

Our front stretched over seventeen English miles and as a result I could not be an eye witness to all of the skirmishes and remember only some. The areas of Virginia are so wooded and muddy that the communications between divisions were hampered. On May 15, we finally stood in an open line in front of the walls around Richmond. General McClellan assured himself communications with the town of Yorktown through Williamsburg and with Fort Monroe and the banks of the York River through White House. The area where we stood, however, was wooded and muddy and I did not know anything about our center column.

We began to besiege the city from two sides, but because of a shortage of reinforcements and siege artillery we could not immediately conquer it. When we began the siege we expected that these reinforcements and artillery would soon arrive from Washington, but we neither anticipated nor understood the intrigue that would be fostered by those who were opposed to McClellan, undeniably one of the most capable generals in the Northern Army.

The speedy march from Yorktown to Richmond behind the retreating Southerners demonstrated to me the energy and enterprise of the Yankees. I must admit that it was very bold and risky because it led to the heart of the enemy's country without a secure line of communications or retreat. Thus, when the Southerners brought significant reinforcements into Richmond, broke our siege lines and attacked our flanks from all sides, we paid for this boldness in blood.

For several weeks we stayed in a muddy area near Richmond, denied all comforts, with the privations becoming so acute that one-fourth of the army became ill and the effective forces shrank from 96,000 to 46,000 fit for battle.[8]

My regiment was again used for police duties. While conducting this duty we had enough time to train in the maneuvers of a soldier. This duty, however, was very fatiguing as a result of the daily training and having to pull sentry and field guard duty at night. Our regiment was made up of foreigners knowing little English and the general of our brigade, an American, did what he could to assign us the most arduous

---

[8]Although McClellan's army was certainly beset by diseases, it also received periodic reinforcements and it is doubtful that his effective force was ever reduced to the extent that Żychliński maintains.

chores, wanting in this way to protect the Irishmen. Commands are given in the English language, but the battalion school and instructions are taken from the French school and translated into English. The use of English for commands created many difficulties for some officers who did not know the language very well, and I often heard my friends memorizing the commands and maneuvers, and examining one another in broken English.

When we did not only pull guard duty, we were used to construct batteries and roads. We were ordered to build trenches and often while working we had to take up arms in order to defend ourselves from the enemy's riflemen who attempted to prevent us from building the trenches and batteries.

When General McClellan decided to lay siege to Richmond, he brought in siege cannons and mortars of a large caliber to bombard the city and the fortifications surrounding it. Every day there took place guerilla skirmishes after which the enemy usually withdrew into his trenches and fortifications. The enemy's artillery fired shells and bombs, lighting up our camps and night posts. General McClellan raised a balloon every two days where, from an extreme height, he could observe the movements and fortifications of the enemy. Once I was an eye witness to this ascent, and I admit that I am deeply amazed by the inventive shrewdness of the Americans. The balloon is silk and quite big. Releasing it, they attach a small rubber gondola in which two people sit. One person releases and directs the balloon and the second is usually an engineering officer who observes the enemy with a telescope and the necessary instruments.[9]

As a result of the poor administration we have food of the worst kind and we constantly live by dry biscuits, salted fatback or salted meats. Because of the muddy area, the water was the worst. It was of a dirty white color like milk mixed with coffee. For five weeks I did not see any fresh bread nor milk. This indescribable poverty annoyed us. Diseases began to appear and the heat was unbearable. Only the officers had tents and the soldiers slept under the open sky come rain or shine.

The muddy region in which we camped, and the rank odors at night, were reasons why we had about 150 sick with fever in some regiments. Typhoid began to appear and thousands of sick soldiers were sent to field hospitals either in Williamsburg, Yorktown or Fort

---

[9] The leader of this project to provide the Union Army with aerial observation was Professor T.S.C. Lowe. Because his first two initials stood for Thaddeus Sobieski, some Polish American writers have given him a Polish identity. There is no evidence to support this contention. Interestingly, among the European observers with McClellan's army was Count von Zeppelin, a German aristocrat and soldier who later became the father of the German airships which bore his name.

Monroe. Our forces began to diminish. The General ordered reinforcements from Washington, but he waited in vain. It was suspected that General McClellan secretly favored the Democratic Party, and because of this he did not possess the confidence of the so-called "Black Republicans," led by President Lincoln and Secretary of State Stanton,[10] the latter of whom had at his side Count Adam Gurowski.[11]

Count Gurowski was a diplomat who had been known at the Court in St. Petersburg. He had to escape from there because of a misunderstanding wherein he compromised himself over the publication of a certain brochure. I knew the Gurowski family in our homeland [Poland] where Count Adam was often kind to me and explained many things, thus facilitating my access to a company of prominent persons in the United States. In this company I could hear opinions on the causes of the Civil War, and find out about the intrigues that England and Napoleon III were conducting on behalf of the Southern states in an attempt to sow discord, break up the Union, and weaken the spread of republican principles in Europe.

On the general staff, and in the army, I also met officers of various nationalities who were veterans of European armies. On General McClellan's staff, in addition to the Comte de Paris, who was the son of the former King Phillippe, was his uncle, the Prince de Joinville who sought to teach his nephew, through practical experience, the art of military science while at the same time demonstrating the political sentiments of the Orleanists toward the United States.[12] During the period of

---

[10]Historians generally believe that President Lincoln and Secretary of War [not "State" as Żychliński indicates] Edwin Stanton provided sufficient support for McClellan's venture against Richmond. They have criticized him for sending some reinforcements to the Shenandoah Valley area which could have been used in the Peninsula Campaign, but the generally accepted conclusion is that McClellan was overly cautious, tended to inflate the size of the enemy's forces which he faced, and used the imagined lack of reinforcements as a convenient excuse to explain his own inadequacies as a commander in the field. After being relieved of command following the Antietam Campaign in the fall of 1862, McClellan ran as the Democratic candidate for President against Lincoln in 1864.

[11]Count Adam Gurowski was an obstinate radical who advocated Pan Slavism and leveled verbal abuse and threats upon anyone who did not agree entirely with his point of view. At one point during the war President Lincoln is said to have remarked that the one person whom he really feared was Count Gurowski. For a full treatment of Gurowski's involvement in the wartime controversies see LeRoy H. Fisher, *Lincoln's Gadfly, Adam Gurowski* (Norman: University of Oklahoma Press, 1964). Gurowski's diaries have also been published and make for very interesting reading.

[12]Many foreign officers came to the United States during the Civil War seeking active commissions in the military forces, while still others came as adventurers to offer their services as volunteer aides, or as official observers representing the military establishment of their native land. The Prince de Joinville, a member of the royal

Napoleon I, my aunt married the Marque de Montpesar, a former general under King Phillippe. Because of this I had letters from my cousins assuring me access, through these princes, to the general staff. I could thus obtain much information which remained a secret to others and which explained to me why we were not quickly sent reinforcements from Washington. The government did not want to entrust more soldiers to the command of General McClellan since his enemies publicly accused him of treason and incompetence. In America there are now two main political parties: one is called the Republican and the second the Democratic. General McClellan belongs to the Democratic Party, whereas the Republican Party, at the head of which stands the President, was against the General, and as is known from the newspapers of June, 1862, relieved him of his command over the whole army. The position of general McClellan was then given to General Halleck.

Among the other Europeans whom I encountered while in the army were former officers of the Russian army. I became acquainted with them, we lived as good friends, and we often fought battles together under the same republican banner. From these Russians I often heard statements that convinced me that the real intellectuals in Russia are not against liberating Poland from under the yoke of absolute Czardom because, they confess, that in suppressing Poland the Russians are placing the manacles of absolutism on their own hands and legs, and as long as Russia is not a constitutional state like the civilizations of the west, it will subjugate civilized Poland and will not assist the Slavs in liberating themselves from German rapacity which seeks to denationalize and subjugate the Slavic tribes for the sake of German culture. I also met, while abroad, the Russian socialist Bakunin,[13] the father of today's revolutionary party in Russia, and the positivist and realist Hercen, editor of *Crocodile*.[14] Often I heard what could assure me that the revolutionary party in Russia, the so-called "Reds," desires to work hand-in-

family of Orleans in France, was one of the more celebrated of these European observers.

[13]Mikhail Aleksandrovich Bakunin (1814-1876) was a Russian anarchist who took an active part in the European revolutionary movements throughout this period. He refused to return to Russia, was expelled from Paris for attempts to incite the overthrow of the monarchy, and sentenced to death by Austria. Eventually captured by the Austrians, he was handed over to the Russian government which exiled him to Siberia. He escaped via Japan to the United States in 1861, and later became a leading anarchist author in Europe where he worked closely with Karl Marx and Friedrich Engels. He was expelled from the First International for his militant views. Eventually his writings led to the establishment of the nihilist movement in Russia.

[14]Aleksandr Ivanovich Herzen (1812-1870) was a leading Russian author and political instigator who lived most of his adult life in London and Paris. *Crocodile* was a periodical which Herzen edited

French officers relax over lunch during the Peninsula Campaign.
Seated, left to right, are Captain Leclerc, the Duc de Chartres,
the Comte de Paris, the Prince de Joinville, and Captain Mohain.
[*Photo from Miller's photographic history of the Civil War*]

hand with the Poles to jointly crush absolutism and the lawlessness of the bureaucracy in Russia, and later, together with the Poles, stand against the Pan Germanism movement now growing in Frankfurt-am-Main. The intelligent Russians are now joining Hercen, while the young and enthusiastic elements surrounded Bakunin and receive nourishment from one who, twenty years later, Czardom would first exile to Siberia and finally send to the gallows. I recall well in England a speech in 1860 given by Louis Blanc[15] at an assembly of delegates of the revolutionary committees in which he argued against Bakunin and maintained that through demoralization Russia can achieve freedom. He condemned nihilism as gangrene in the revolutionary body. Hercen did not agree with Bakunin's theories, nor did he had close contact with the Poles. Both, however, wanted to use the Poles to fight absolutism in Russia, and both desired a social revolution there.

In the army of the United States, all social and revolutionary elements were present and often the officers assembled during their free time to discuss the best means by which the republican spirit could be transplanted from America to Europe, and how it was necessary to ensure the freedom and independence of the subjugated nations. Always at these disputes the most extreme opinions were displayed by the French and the Russians. They regarded us Poles as conservatives, obscurants, bigots, and completely incapable of comprehending a true social revolution through which alone Europe can overcome monarchism, the hegemony of might over right, and the suppression of labor by capital. Since that time twenty long and painful years have gone by. However, I remember very well that this is the same philosophy that socialist France, Germany and Russia are writing about and implementing today. Already, twenty years ago, a program was in place to conduct this battle for social revolution. But, let us now return to our activities before Richmond.

On June 18, I commanded the guards and the outpost of our regiment in the vicinity of the battery we formed. Unaccustomed to such meager rations and the changing climate of Virginia, I came down with ague, but I performed my duty as best I could. Since I spoke English well, Colonel Confort usually sent me to important outposts. On that night, June 18, around 2:00 a.m., an alert went off near my post. Having found out from the staff officer that the enemy was approaching in my direction in several columns. I broke post and returned to the regiment, which was formed in columns, and we were sent three can-

---

[15]Jean Joseph Charles Louis Blanc (1811-1882) is regarded as the founder of state socialism. A French journalist, he attacked the policies of the government of Louis Phillippe and served in the provincial revolutionary government of 1848.

nons to support us. After giving a report, I joined my unit, Company E, which consisted of 42 people, where I waited for commands.[16]

We stood for quite a long while without orders until we received instructions to advance as quickly as possible to the left wing of the brigade and support our position there until further orders. The colonel, wanting to occupy his position as quickly as possible, ordered us to advance at double time, and finally to trot. He forgot that having a forest in front of us we could not run in tight columns and maintain ranks. After entering the forest, chaos and disorder erupted in the columns of untrained soldiers. However, fortunately, I can say that in this chaos the enemy did not attack us and the darkness shielded our ignominious disgrace since the enemy could not see the confusion and disorder. During this confusion I fell with my whole pack and weight on a tree stump and several soldiers from my platoon fell on top of me. At first I lost consciousness. Then I was able to stand with the aid of some soldiers, but I noticed that I could only walk with pain and difficulty. Necessity forced me to use all my strength to stand in my assigned place. I commanded the third platoon in the company and I needed to form the first two platoons, which in the confusion went to Company F. After quite a long time of urging and giving commands, I formed my platoon again and joined the center of the regiment where rifle fire already began to light up the darkness surrounding us. We just formed a group in the forest when the enemy, informed of our presence from the cries of commands and signals of the bugler, greeted us with battalion fire and soon attacked us with bayonets.

The young, and inexperienced soldiers in the center held back the onslaught of the enemy's first charge, however, the right and left wing completely broke and began to retreat in disorder. Our whole regiment certainly would have been taken prisoner if the three cannons standing behind us had not effectively greeted the enemy with a rain of grapeshot and shrapnel. The enemy, believing that our side had a larger force, began to retreat and allowed us to regroup into a line of battle once again. In this skirmish we lost 31 killed, with 79 wounded. I myself took a bayonet wound, but it was nothing significant.

The next day fever and fatigue so weakened me that I had to submit my name to the sick-call list for the hospital and was taken to Williamsburg where for one hot week I laid in a tent and became worse. The doctor sent me to Yorktown where I would be more comfortable. From

---

[16]The Company E Descriptive Book for the *Enfans Perdu,* on file in the National Archives, indicate that Żychliński was enrolled as 5th Sergeant in Comapny E on April 18, 1862, and transferred as Sergeant to Company B on April 26 of the same year. Unfortunately, the descriptive book for Company B has not survived.

my heavy fall on June 18, a rupture appeared and so pained me that the doctors feared that gangrene might set in. In this hospital in Yorktown, where 3,200 wounded and sick lay, one could not find any leeches or ice. I was in the most terrible state and I myself did not know how I could survive the fever in such extreme heat and discomfort for more than three weeks.

During the time of my illness, the worst kind of news was reaching us from the army of General McClellan near Richmond. The enemy defeated McClellan's army at all points and news came to us that the enemy was marching on Yorktown.[17] Because of this message the order went out for all sick and wounded lying in Yorktown to be sent to various ports in the North. Yorktown lies on the banks of the York River and steamships were leaving every day for Washington and New York.

Doctors began to examine the sick under the personnel super-vision of the chief surgeon of the army, General Dix, who commanded Fort Monroe and a division near Yorktown. During the examination, the doctor, seeing that my rupture, proclaimed me unfit for further duty, gave me a certificate, and sent me to a hospital in Baltimore, Maryland with yet more sick and wounded. After a thirty-hour voyage I finally arrived in Baltimore weakened and suffering. The hospitals were already so overcrowded that they transported us outside of town and placed us in tents where soldiers with typhoid fever were lying. The manner in which the sick and the wounded were treated was barbaric, without any delicateness or service. We were not even asked if we wanted to drink or eat.

The inhabitants of the town of Baltimore did not support the government of the United States because, in general, all of Maryland supports the Confederacy. The inhabitants of Baltimore hate the Northern soldiers. They received us, the sick and wounded, without any sympathy or mercy and of course swore and reviled us. They asked us if we had enough patriotism for the government of the United States.

Two soldiers carried me from the ship and I asked to be taken to the nearest hotel where, having regained my spirit, I gathered all my strength and wrote to New York describing my position to my friend living there. This friend came personally and offered me his house for a time until I got better. I willingly accepted his friendly offer. After arranging my formal matters, I was discharged on the third day. I was also paid for my four months of service and given a certificate stating that because of my rupture I was permanently unfit for further service,

---

[17]McClellan's Peninsula Campaign ended in disaster with a series of defeats by a smaller Southern army during Seven Days' Battle. Only a desperate stand at Malvern Hill allowed McClellan's army to escape destruction.

Battalion return for July, 1862,
showing Żychliński as discharged for disability.
[*Courtesy of the National Archives*]

and at the same time I was freed from my pledge of loyalty to the United States as a soldier.[18]

On July 8, 1862, I left Baltimore with the aid of two soldiers assigned to me. On July 10, I arrived at the house of my friend in New York and as I entered the doctors immediately began healing me. I suffered through two weeks without a change of food, a comfortable bed or the attempts of my friends to get me on my feet. I was weak and did not have any strength and the doctors forbade me to go outside for a whole month.

Today [1862] I feel healthy and am ready again to serve my fatherland if, in time, it needs me. I work here for my keep either by writing or manual labor. My wound, which will always be a reminder to me of my American campaign, did not allow me to walk fast and every day I walked with difficulty to the town library in Boston where, reading newspapers, magazines, and interesting works, I think about current events and politics of North America.

What I have described above is a short account of my arrival in this country and my four months of active duty in the army. I described facts and events seen personally and the course of their military organization in general. I did not want to pass judgment on the faults of the generals and administration or politics of such an unfortunate country that is crumbling from such a bloody fratricidal war.

---

[18]The battalion return for the *Enfans Perdu* for July, 1862, indicates that Żychliński was discharged for disability on July 11, 1862. The battalion muster roll for June 30-August 31, 1862, lists him as "Discharged for disability at Yorktown, Va., on July 11, 1862."

Chapter 4

Life in the Army

Following induction into the ranks of the United States army, there began for me a life full of impressions and adventures which I will describe here so that the reader may see not only the camp life of the soldier but the society of the entire country in which Europeans meet surprises and see themselves in a magic circle.[1] Since everything was different in the New World, ideas were also different than in Europe. Customs and views were different and completely new. Everywhere one can meet this spirit of progress; a hardworking drive and purely republican sentiment. Freedom and the equality of citizens were also applied, and after service in the ranks they revealed themselves in almost every soldier. The subordination and military discipline within the service were so exemplary they could even serve as a model for the Prussian army. After the service we were all equal and free citizens who, of our own volition, enlisted in the army and submitted to the discipline in order to fight the enemy who threatened the republic's existence and freedom. It was already apparent then that England was aiding the Southern rebellion in order to weaken the government in Washington. In France, Napoleon III also favored the South because he desired to

---

[1]The material from this point on is exclusively from Żychliński's memoirs penned after the war. In this chapter there is some repetition as he recounts many of the events already discussed in his 1862 memoir, but the reader should take note of some subtle differences and the temporizing of some of his views about the punish-ment for embezzlement, the chances for a Northern victory, and so on, as he looks back on these events after the passage of many years.

establish in Mexico a dynasty which the United States could not thwart while embroiled in such a bloody civil war.[2]

The beginning of this war was not advantageous for the Northern states because in the Southern states there were many former officers and generals from the regular army of the United States, which numbered only 16,000 soldiers, together with other combative elements and hard working planters and slave owners. In contrast, the Northern states had to hastily organize an army composed of volunteers who were largely unaccustomed to soldiering. Officers and generals of this volunteer army were inexperienced and had to learn on the battlefields.[3] It is an irrefutable fact that if the Southern states had, immediately at the beginning of the war, quickly attacked Washington with the armed forces they possessed, the Southerners would, without fail, have conquered the town and the war would have taken a completely different turn. Then the principle of slavery would certainly have prevailed for an indefinite time across the ocean. Our numerical and material means were so much greater than in the rebellious states.[4] With these means they organized in the Northern states an enormous army made up of volunteers. They managed at the beginning of the war, despite the shortage off their own professional officers, by accepting from Europe newcomers and military men of various nationalities and caliber who were paid a high price. These men had before them a wartime career and the promise of future upkeep and, in the event that they were wounded, they were guaranteed a life-time pension.

A complete lack of competent officers on the general staff was the weakness of the Northern army, and the lack of artillery officers was especially felt at the beginning of the war. In addition to this, each state

---

[2]Throughout the war, the English and French governments remained generally supportive of the Confederates. The English sold goods to the South, outfitted Southern privateers, and became so blatant in their support of the secessionist movement that an international tribunal convened after the conclusion of the war awarded the United States some $15,500,000 in reparations. The French, who were even more openly supportive of the South than were the English, attempted to take advantage of American preoccupation with the Civil War to establish a French Empire in Mexico. Napoleon III sent French troops into Mexico to support the Austrian Archduke Maximilian as Emperor of Mexico. In May, 1865, following the surrender of the main Confederate armies, 50,000 United States troops were sent to the Mexican border and Napoleon eventually withdrew his forces in May, 1866.

[3]Popular mythology has long held that the South was successful at the beginning of the war largely because so many West Point-trained officers resigned to serve in the Confederate armies. Actually, only about one West Point-trained officer in five went South, and for the most part the main armies on both sides were led by West Pointers throughout the war.

[4]The North possessed enormous advantages in factories, bank deposits, population, raw materials, and even in the production of food products.

was to supply a quota of troops to the central government, a task that met with great difficulties because they had to enlist volunteers to fill the army. For this reason they began to give volunteers a $100 bonus, and finally they provided a $500 bounty, with the remuneration paid in advance to volunteers recruited for the duration of the war. Such volunteers from cities were not trained and often they had to be sent into the battle lines while not adequately acquainted even with the use of their weapons. They were often useless to the army, but were not spared and were led into battles with real American disregard for the murderous fire. Many officers were lacking in military training and only knew how to bravely lead often disordered columns into the attack with disregard for the lives of their subordinates.

They also fought bloody battles there, and in addition many soldiers and officers died of various diseases because the field hospitals were not adequately and properly equipped. The shortage of doctors always seemed so glaring that often the wounded and sick remained whole days without the necessary dressing.

The murderous climate decimated the wounded as well as the sick. All of this, however, did not stop the enterprising Yankees. Every day the army grew and improved so much more. Officers and leaders obtained practical experience on the battlefield and became much more skilled. Among them, those with abilities were uncovered and slowly surfaced to assume the mantel of authority. At the end of the war the Americans could do without the European officers, and even surpassed them and disregarded their services.

In the army of the United States true service and skill easily found recognition because after each battle a war commission composed of members of Congress discussed the activities of the officers and leaders and through its judgment provided punishment or rewards. Also, influence did not have any meaning there, and only personal worth and skill could decide on an advance and the promoting of officers and generals to higher positions.[5] They have no military orders and decorations in America, the only rewards for acts of courage and service on the battlefield being public announcements of appreciation placed in the newspapers or written in books, and monetary rewards.[6] To insure subordina-

---

[5]Although it was possible to rise through "personal worth and skill," many commissions were obtained through political influence, recruiting, or other means unassociated with military expertise. Note the difference between these comments, penned long after the end of the Civil War, and his observations about the bounty system and recruitment of regiments in Chapter 2, written in 1862.

[6]The Medal of Honor was authorized by Congress in December, 1861, several individual officers or units issued their own commemorative medals, and Congress also authorized several special medals during the war. The standard method of recognition

tion and discipline in the ranks of the armies standing on the battle line in the face of the enemy there were severe punishments prescribed by laws passed in Congress. The death penalty for those condemned by court martial was executed quickly because there was no means of clemency for those crimes which were by law marked for the death penalty.

The organization of the volunteer regiment took place in a purely democratic manner. Soldiers elected officers, and the colonel named the non-commissioned officers. He was appointed by the governor of a state and, along with the other officers of the regiment, confirmed by the Secretary of War. The volunteer regiments began to form when the governor of a state gave permission to citizens known for their honesty and republican patriotism to assemble and recruit a regiment. Thus appointed, these colonels would find a major and captains who became responsible to him for recruiting volunteers. Captains and majors sought officers who themselves became obligated to recruit soldiers for them. Each of these would-be officers searched and recruited, and after gathering a sufficient quantity of men they were chosen as officers in the regiment. Soon, when the governor was informed that the regiment was assembled, he provided nominations which were then usually confirmed by the War Department. Afterwards the regiment swore loyalty to the central government in Washington and entered the list of armies. From that time on, the cost of supporting the regiment was borne by the War Department. For this reason, everywhere on the street, in the tap rooms, cafes, and restaurants, volunteers were recruited with promises of mountains of gold, comforts, assurances of safety from enemy bullets, ample financial offerings, and remuneration both before and after the war. As further inducement, the prospective volunteers were often offered free meals and plied with liquor. Each recruiting agent made exaggerated promises. All of these various recruiting maneuvers appeared to me to be just like the ridiculously exaggerated claims of a Jewish tradesman praising his goods and his honesty because of the stiff competition for this product. I often saw bloody episodes in which one and the same volunteer, taking generous pledges from several recruiters at once, was beaten within an inch of his life by the recruiters. They conducted a volunteer to an office where a doctor examined him. If he was capable of military service the doctor gave him a certificate. Afterwards they gave him a so-called account from which he personally acknowledged receipt and was immediately sworn in. Then they took him to the headquarters of the assembled regiment, company, or battal-

---

was, however, as Żychliński suggests, announcement of a person's name in the official battle reports and newspapers.

ion. The regiment was made up of two battalions each consisting of five hundred people. The Secretary of War received the allegiance of the volunteers, gave them a standard and arms, confirmed nominations, and immediately sent them to their designated brigade in the field. There, since they were usually but poorly trained, they were properly schooled and drilled to meet the enemy. Often, several days after its arrival on the battlefield, a regiment would engage in skirmishes and would be sent into bloody battles.[7]

For the cost of recruiting, housing, and feeding the assembled recruits while they were being organized, the colonel received state money from which he had to account for expenses. And at the same time, also at the cost of the state, he received clothes, underwear, and uniforms for the enlisted volunteers. Also, each state was assigned a quota of soldiers which it was obligated to raise, with the quota being determined by the number of troops which Congress voted to raise. Some states had great difficulty supplying volunteers and were forced to provide a financial bounty in order to supply the prescribed number of troops to the War Department. Because of this there were various opportunities for abuse and swindling, and often there were more soldiers on paper than actually stood in the ranks during battle.

Although the central government assigned officers to each state to oversee and control the acquisition of supplies for the army, nevertheless, often regiments which were supposed to number 1,000 men in their ranks had only 600 or 800 at the most. The rest were entered on the rolls as sick, wounded, or detailed to a recruiting company, a unit which was responsible for filling newly created gaps in the ranks. It was obligated to send fresh recruits straight to its regiment in the front lines. Any person who had connections with the authorities of a state, and financial resources, could recruit volunteers. If someone collected the prescribed quantity of soldiers, he could become a colonel, major, captain, first lieutenant, or second lieutenant. In this way our fellow countrymen Krzyżanowski, Rosencrantz, Szeinic,[8] and others were able

---

[7]Though seemingly a comic opera, the description of the manner in which officers were appointed and regiments recruited is generally correct.

[8]Włodzimierz B. Krzyżanowski, an exile from the Mierosławski insurrection of 1846, was appointed colonel of the 58th New York Infantry, generally known as the "Polish Legion," which he raised from among the immigrant population in New York City. He fought at Cross Keys where he was cited for gallantry, and was then given a brigade which he led at Second Bull Run, Chancellorsville and Gettysburg. He was promoted to the rank of brigadier general on March 2, 1865. See James S. Pula, *For Liberty and Justice: The Life and Times of Wladimir Krzyżanowski* (Chicago: Polish American Congress Charitable Foundation, 1978).

The reference to Rosencrantz is most likely Palle Rosencrantz, a former colonel in the Swedish Army who commanded a small corps in West Virginia, and was for two

to arrive in the United States at the beginning of the war and enter the volunteer army as colonels. They seemed to be competent military men and rendered services on the battlefield, eventually becoming generals. After the conclusion of the war, Krzyżanowski and Rosencrantz were even accepted into the regular army and remain continuously on duty until today.[9] Those who lacked financial resources and contacts, regardless of their capabilities as a professional officers, entered the volunteer army as a non-commissioned officer or second lieutenant and could only advance through conduct on the battlefield, which often occurred only with great difficulty. At the beginning of the war some officers from European armies were accepted into the regular army or staff by the War Department. This was especially true of artillery officers or general staff, but it was necessary to have great influence and ability in order to be accepted into the regular army of 40,000 soldiers. There thus appeared little chance of advancement because the authorities preferred the native-born over foreigners. After 1862 no foreign officers were allowed into the regular army because the ranks were supplied with competent officers from the volunteer army.

As for me, I succeeded in April [1862] in being accepted onto the staff as an officer. But after resigning from the army in April, 1863, to serve in the Polish uprising, I was dropped from the ranks of the army, forfeited the right of advancement, lost pay that was due for having received wounds, and also permanently lost all rights vested in me as a citizen of the United States.[10] In 1863, many of the Poles wanted to leave the United States army to serve in the [Polish] uprising. But, being aware of the consequences that would result from such resignation from the army, they remained in the ranks throughout the remainder of the war. Nevertheless, despite great difficulty, several of us were able to leave America in April [1863] to rush to Europe where we were

years a major in the 4th New York Cavalry. It is also possible that it may refer to Frederick Anton Ulrik Rosencrantz, a captain in the Royal Life Guards of Sweden, who enlisted in the German Turner Regiment in New York in 1861. He finished the war as a brevet lieutenant colonel for services rendered during the Siege of Richmond and Petersburg and the Appomattox Campaign.

The reference to Szeinic is unknown.

[9]Krzyżanowski served briefly as military commander in northern Alabama, and was then appointed as a federal treasury agent serving at various times in the Reconstruction governments of the South, the Washington Territory, Alaska, Panama, and New York City. There is no evidence that he ever held a commission in the regular army.

[10]Żychliński's claims to have resigned in May, 1863, to fight in the 1863 uprising in Poland and several Polish sources confirm his participation in that conflict. For a discussion of this, and the uncertainty of his whereabouts from fall, 1862, through May, 1863, see the introduction to this work.

called by our obligation as loyal sons of Poland and the further desire to measure ourselves on the battlefield with the butchers and murderers of our grandfathers, fathers, and brothers.

At that time it was already a foregone conclusion that the Northern states were defeating the South, and that they would maintain the Union and completely abolish slavery. In 1863 we already had an entire volunteer regiment recruited completely from Negroes. The Southern armies were surrounded in a tight circle by an army of 800,000 persistent and enterprising Yankees from the Northern states. Officers and soldiers alike had tents made from thick cotton sailing cloth, and even an army living in camp outside a town or village was not quartered there because the citizens were free from any requirement to quarter troops. This right was respected even in enemy territory. Soldiers, whether officers or common enlisted men, coming from camp to town or village could not carry any arms in order not to restrict in any way the personal freedom of the citizens. They only carried their arms while on duty, when they were in the ranks, on guard, or going under a written order in the interest of duty. Even while on duty, officers were not allowed to walk among citizens on the street with a sword at their side. Even the generals stayed in tents while in camps, although nearby there might be found comfortable quarters. If they were settled in some kind of quarters, they did this with a hospitable invitation or rented a quarter by voluntary agreement. Also, the temporary field hospitals of the camps were located in tents, usually behind towns or charitable societies formed by private citizens who took the wounded into their homes, or to special places arranged for that purpose. The personal freedom of citizens was respected everywhere. Their personal property was untouchable because the purpose of the army was not to restrict the freedom of the citizens, but to protect them from the enemy. For this, it was paid and well supplied in needs and food by the nation.

At the beginning of the month, or quarterly, officers received their pay with ready cash, as did the soldiers. The soldiers also received food and clothing. Officers had to buy themselves food and hire servants by volunteer agreement and pay in the ranks. Finally, the officers also had to buy themselves, from the pay which they received, a field cap. This could be done from either private suppliers or government warehouses, or it could be obtained on credit from the warehouse. The cost of the product chosen was deducted by officers called paymasters. This paymaster, upon the paying of wages, showed each officer his individual debts in the account book.

Such manipulations were very convenient for the government, but for the officers it was very inconvenient and burdensome, especially during marches in the heart of an unfriendly and destroyed country because one could not always take with himself supplies, provisions and forage for the horses. To be sure, with each battalion and regiment there was a so called sutler, a camp following merchant who was obligated to haul behind the army all things needed for food and the convenience of the officers and soldiers. But such camp merchants could not always keep pace with the army. As a result, officers often had to buy needed provisions from soldiers at exorbitant prices. Soldiers up to the rank of sergeant major in the cavalry and sergeant in the infantry took their rations in common. Each company or troop received provisions individually from the government field warehouse. Whereas rations were abundant, officers could eat with the soldiers at an agreed price. Often this caused difficulties because on the front lines in face of the enemy there was a shortage of wagons to transport provisions in sufficient quantities. Often after a couple of days the soldiers did not collect their full rations. For these shortages, after calculations, they were scrupulously paid in cash. The soldier had to collect the ration of food allotted to him by Congress. In addition he looked after his rations so that he would not be denied those to which he was rightfully entitled.

The soldier collected ground coffee, sugar, pressed vegetables, salt, molasses, meat, dry biscuits, or wheat bread, cereal, grits, lard fat and even vinegar from the field warehouse. He acknowledged receipt of these rations, and of the quantity received, from the warehouse. On the other hand, if there was a dearth of something due him, then he had the right to demand money for this in accordance with the price assigned on each object and article by an established commission of experts. Injustice to a soldier in regard to his rations or even his clothes is not tolerated. Moreover, if the products were bad or spoiled the soldier could immediately write in his complaint. In this way no one was ever threatened with abuses by the authorities. A commission formed from delegates of Congress toured the camps and armies and severely punished each abuse of the authorities and injustice of a soldier or officer.[11]

To collect rations from the warehouses, the soldiers in the company vote for delegates who went daily to obtain the company's provisions and sign in an account book for the amount of the products taken. In this way control was also kept and neither the warehouse nor the soldier could be cheated in any way. The soldiers received their rations from these delegates, and when there was a shortage of something they

---

[11]While in camp, the Northern troops generally ate well. In the field, however, there were chronic shortages due to transportation difficulties and other logistical problems associated with provisioning a mobile army in the course of a campaign. Often the diet consisted on nothing more than hardtack and *ersatz* coffee made from roasting corn for days at a time. Dysentery and other diseases which resulted from this nutritional nightmare claimed more lives than did Confederate bullets.

immediately noted this in books listing what was lacking or the quantity. It was the same with receipt of clothing, underwear and shoes which were assigned to each soldier for a certain period of time. If, on the other hand, a soldier took some kind of clothing wear ahead of time he had to pay for this by deductions from his pay. Sometimes the paymaster did not bring the pay to the battle line for three months, but no one lost anything by this and even after death the money belonging to the soldier was sent to the family in a receipt that could be cashed in a bank.

The same happened with the wounded. The regulations there were exemplary and conscientiously upheld because control remained in the hands of the interested persons, unlike other armies where it was in the hands of the exploiters who cared little about the comfort and needs of the soldiers. This frequently happened in Europe where soldiers usually fought for foreign causes, and not their own. The paymasters did not belong to the military authority. They were civilian treasury clerks and had to place the pay in the hands of the soldiers themselves, not in the hands of the captains as is the practice in the European armies.

There were indeed abuses because where there are people abuses must take place. But always the soldier of the United States had an open opportunity to complain to higher authority. No one had the right to obstruct his access to the leader and to the highest authority which was obligated to receive and settle the just complaints of the subordinates.

Such difference in the Republic of the United States of America discerns the soldiers and the free citizens from the soldiers of the monarchial governments in Europe, and because of this it is not surprising that the army of the United States found millions of volunteers in its ranks during the long and bloody Civil War. There was no compulsory service.[12] However, they raised in the ranks an army of a million strong made up of volunteers. They fought a strong and tenacious enemy who was all the more dangerous in defence of a homeland that occupied a large area of undeveloped space that was crowded with enormous obstacles for a free march of numerous columns, and thus difficult to conquer.

The entire army was a model of rigor and subordination, especially in the ranks in face of the enemy. Punishments for each infraction were decided by Congress, and were read to the soldiers and officers. Once they volunteered, both soldiers and officers had to submit to these regu-

---

[12]While the vast majority of soldiers who served on both sides during the Civil War were volunteers, both North and South also passed conscription laws to encourage volunteering and make up for short-falls in recruiting. The first Southern conscription act was passed on April 16, 1862, while the Northern Congress enacted the Enrollment Act on March 3, 1863.

lations. Orders in the army were scrupulously executed because each disobedience or breaking of the law was most severely punished. For those infractions on the battle lines the punishment of death was meted out. The military court met for only a few hours, and the sentences were carried out immediately because there was no road for mercy for these crimes. Friends judged the accused and announced if he was guilty or not guilty. The authorities, according to military law, set the punishment and saw to the execution of the sentence. The accused could defend himself, could request a defender, and could summon witnesses in his own defense, but he could not prolong his defense nor the execution of the sentence. If he was caught red-handed in a crime, then two hours after committing the crime he was judged and punished. There was only one means of help for the accused and that was if the whole company unanimously recognized him as innocent and demanded his freedom, which happened very rarely. This is because the feeling of justice and fairness is deeply rooted in the society of the United States of North America and therefore a culprit always receives a fair punishment.

I am mentioning here a certain crime committed by a soldier on the battlefield in enemy country in Virginia of which I was an eye witness. This example will illustrate the kind of severity and subordination that was maintained in the ranks of an army made up of volunteers and how they showed respect for the property of others because it is irrefutable that respect for the property of others is the basis of freedom and each society must uphold this principle if it desires to be free either spiritually, personally, politically, or physically.

We stood in camp in the state of Virginia several miles away from the enemy. Under the punishment of death no one was allowed to take possession of anything that was property of a citizen, nor enter the homes of the inhabitants for the purpose of extortion of any kind, even from a defenseless enemy, and especially from those citizens who do not actively take part in any battle against us.

One day they sent from a regiment coming from New York, and made up for the most part from Europeans, mainly Irishmen and Germans, a company as a vanguard in a distant point about five kilometers from the main camp to observe on that side the movements of the advance guard of the enemy. In the vicinity of the camp of this advance guard several hundred steps away stood farm buildings and the living quarters of the planter in which remained several women, two old people, and several faithful Negroes who did not escape from their former masters. However, the owner of this farm and his sons, together with the white servants, were themselves in the enemy's ranks. We found out about this from the Negroes. At night a fat sow from this farm wandered near the field where the advance guard was camped. The soldiers were hungry for fresh pork. Therefore, several of them grabbed the sow and, having butchered it with bayonets, cut it into pieces, cooked it over a fire and then merrily ate. However, the officers did not know anything about this and only thought that the German and Irish soldiers bought themselves the porkling. In the morning people came from the farm looking for the sow. They noticed the remains and knew that it had been captured and eaten by the Yankees. Immediately the lady of the house went to the camp and denounced the soldiers to the commanding general and demanded compensation and punishment according to the law. I was present at the general's with a report when this woman lodged the complaint. Therefore, I quickly sent by horse a trusted soldier, a Frenchman, to tell this to the commanding officer of the rear guard and request that he order the soldiers to bury and dispose of all traces of this unworthy deed and not to admit fault. From the camp, however, a commission had to go to the place to confirm the complaint.

The messenger did not find the company because it had been relieved by another after a twenty-four-hour guard, and when the captain of the new company heard what had happened he did not want to know anything about this, nor did he want to destroy the criminal evidence. This was a pure-blooded American looking with an ill-disposed eye at foreigners and, in spirit, he was assuredly satisfied that the punishment of death would not touch an American company, but one made up of Europeans. This is how I foresaw what happened because the general sent a commission to the place and also commanded me there, as I was familiar with the French and German languages, to conduct the investigation.

Having arrived at the place I found traces of the crime because the bones, skin, and hooves lay by the fires and the remains were recognized by the lady proprietor and her people as coming from that sow. Immediately a formal account was written. On the other hand, I harshly upbraided the commander of the rear guard for not giving the order to get rid of the traces. If we had not found anything at the place, everything could be denied by the soldiers and the plaintiff could not introduce any proof. Also, the general himself apparently desired to erase this deed because with his eyes he authorized me to warn the rear guard and with serious thought he delegated that for this investigation that I cover up this deed and save a few people from certain death.

When I returned to camp, and after submitting a report to the general, the accused were placed under guard and led to the main quarters. It appeared that seven soldiers took part in catching the sow, but in the whole operation twenty-two soldiers and three non-commissioned officers took part. They all confessed guilt to this. The military court met and granted the accused a defense and at the same time they picked twelve jurors from another company who had to find them either innocent or guilty. I defended the accused as much as I could as their chosen defender, but the mitigating circumstances of the deed had little affect on this because the law clearly sets the penalty of death for such a crime. The prosecuting attorney, a native-born American, put forth the death penalty and the military court agreed to this. The verdict came to executing the seven soldiers, reducing the rank of the non-commissioned officers, and paying back the lady proprietor of the sow because they took part in consuming the stolen object. The rest of the soldiers were condemned to sever punishment in the following manner: carrying packs in parades, confinement to their tents after duty for three months, and the loss of advancement throughout the whole war. The death sentence was carried out in a period of several hours beyond the perimeter of the camp. The next day in the order of the day they mentioned the reasons for such sever punishment and they mentioned that republican soldiers should show respect for a citizen's property and freedom, and that even in the enemy's country he should maintain respect for these ideas and principles for which he is fighting.

The second instance I personally witnessed of the severity of republican laws in the army was during the time that we stood by the sea in the enemy state of Florida. There, while unloading food and ammunition from the ships, three soldiers disguised as deck hands wanted to desert on these same ships, which were scheduled to sail to Havana. These were merchant ships hired by the ministry of war for transporting supplies to the army near the sea in the states of Florida and the Carolinas. However, before the ships raised their anchors, the escape of the three soldiers was noticed in camp. They sent a boat to the ships to search out the deserters and bring them back. The military court met immediately and, according to law, in a period of two hours they were found guilty, sentenced to death, and shot. In the republican army deserters and spies were shot in the back, not the front.

Yet another time during the morning, after being paid at the headquarters for my services, I saw there a certain general going to the person commanding our corps. He was called from Fort Monroe situated at the mouth of the James River. However, in the afternoon I saw this same general led under guard with a ball-and-chain attached to his legs and the emblems of his general's rank torn from his uniform. I asked about the reason for such a sudden change and found out that this general was sentenced to prison for embezzlement of supplies and public accounts.

Such firm justice, and punishment that was meted out, naturally had to exert a good influence in the army. Thus, there was blind obedience to the authorities. And woe be to the general who would break this control and not consider each simple soldier as his fellow citizen, equal in face of the law. It was allowable to punish subordinates by death or other severe punishment for breaking the laws, but officers were strongly prohibited from physically abusing soldiers.

Officers from the European armies, and especially the Prussians and the Russians, did not like the customs in the army of the United States and could not accept that after completing his service the soldier was equal to them as a citizen. After completing his service it was necessary to completely treat him as an equal friend. As a result, no American wanted to serve under a European officer where he would be only a high-paid servant. Only newly arrived soldiers from Europe agreed to be servants because from childhood they were accustomed to tolerating the whims of these lords. Such servants earned $20 or $30 dollars monthly compensation besides the regular pay and rations from the government. Finding servants to clean horses, clothing, and perform other services was the most difficult job for an officer, and not everyone was as lucky as I who found a Pole from the Sultan's cossacks from the time of the Crimean War. He came from the estate of my relative in Wielkopolska, and had been in America since 1857 when he came as a worker. At the beginning of the war he immediately enlisted in the volunteer army in New York State. Because he did not know how to write nor read, he was, therefore, only a private. This good soul pined for his homeland. Having found out that I was a Pole, and in addition to this from Wielkopolska, he came to see me and did not want to part with me. However, he fell, hit with a bullet in the middle of the forehead in the battle of Fredricksburg. During this time I was on the battle line and he looked for me in order to bring me food. I could not find his body. This faithful comrade had the day before a premonition that he would perish in battle. He asked me to write to his family near Września and send money there which he had sewed in the top of his knee boot. I did not want to do this, stating that since he would not be in the battle it was only I who could perish and it would be me, and not him, who would be buried on American soil. Going to the battlefield I happily bid him farewell and recommended that he look after my things and my tent. However, he sincerely cried and said that he had a premonition that he would not see me again. When I gave him a little of my money to save, he did not want to take it and obstinately said that he would not see his family nest and Poland again. After twenty-four hours of battle, seeing that I did not return, he went to the commander of the camp and requested that he be allowed to look for and bring me some food and a warm blanket. He received permission for this and while looking for me on the front battle line the poor soul was shot in the forehead, as told to me by someone in the ambulance service. However, I could not find his body nor the several hundred dollars sown in the top of his boots as they immediately buried the bodies in their uniforms at night on the battle field because the penalty of death awaited each person who robbed the fallen soldier. They only took from the dead their papers. His valuables were given to the commander of the burial detail. This same fate met many because the leaders of the army of the United States did not feel sorry for soldiers during battles when it was necessary to hold an important position or take it from the enemy. They did not mourn human life, but squandered it with complete disregard because they governed themselves on the principle that half measures would not win the war. Nevertheless, they considered war an evil which was necessary to finish radically and quickly.

The Southerners in regard to numbers were in the minority. Their soldiers and officers were poorly dressed and they had worse arms. But in spite of this they had capable and brave leaders. The Southern officers were steadfast, more capable, and burned with hate for, as they called us, "the Yankees." In the Southern army there were quite a significant number of Poles. It seemed to me that fighting in a certain battle against the division of General Pac,[13] we took prisoner quite a few Poles serving in the cavalry who were much amazed when I spoke Polish to them and upbraided them on how they could serve a cause so debased and in defense of slavery. They explained that the war found them in the Southern states and being poor they had to enlist in the army. But they would willingly enter into the ranks of the United States, and they gave a promise that they would not again fight against the army of the Northern states. I helped them gain their freedom and they were sent to General Krzyżanowski, who at that time led a division. He accepted them into his ranks. What happened to them I did not find out because on April 20, 1863, I left the ranks of the United States in order to take part in the uprising and in this way to pay my debt to the Fatherland.

---

[13]The reference to "General Pac" is unknown.

Chapter 5

An Encounter with Indians

Here I will recall that each soldier who enlisted in the army of the Northern States was to receive at the end of the war $100 and 100 acres of land in the east where the government owned large areas of land and forests which remained untilled after the wild Indians were removed from there, and with whom the Americans really acted like barbarians destroying them with swords and inducing them to drink hot and often poisonous drinks which these former masters of America like immensely. Because of this they degenerated and abandoned former noble virtues and dignity.

Recollecting the Indians, I consider it necessary to describe adventures which allowed me to become closer acquainted with the Indians, which at the same time will allow the reader to clearly recognize in what kind of untamed country we often had to conduct war and to what inconveniences and dangers our mobile columns were exposed as they often ventured deep into the wild country in order to inspect and reconnoiter the enemy's positions.

In June, 1863, I was sent with a mobile column composed of 500 infantry, 250 cavalry, and four light artillery guns under the leadership of General MacDonald[1] to reconnoiter the armed forces of the South-

---

[1]According to other portions of his memoir, he cliamed to have left for Poland in May, 1863, thus the date of these events must be in error. William F. Amann's *Personnel of the Civil War* (New York: Thomas Yoseloff, 1961) lists over 2,500 persons who held either full or brevet ranks of general in the Union Army during the Civil War. The surname MacDonald does not appear. Further, an examination of the available records of the *Enfans Perdu*, and subsequent secondary sources, indicates no service other than in Virginia, the Carolinas, and Florida. For a discussion of this mystery, see the introduction to this work.

erners toward the Missouri River near the town of St. Louis. Our march took place in an unpopulated area of swamps and pristine forests where there were no suitable roads. A small tribe of Indians acted as our guides. They led us beyond the rear of an army of Southerners dispersed behind St. Louis, but we were not able to find out anything certain about their strength and position. The population, however, was very unfriendly to the Yankees and it was not possible to find any spies.

The appearance of mobile columns behind the enemy's lines forced him to change his defensive position, and at various times his whole battle line. At the same time, it provided the possibility of exact recognition of the enemy's strength and his position. Because of this, one can execute the appropriate plan of attack. This marks the enemy's center of gravity which, once conquered, would force the enemy to fight a pitched battle in a disadvantageous position or retreat further into the seceding states. The mission of the Northern army was to restrict the enemy's movement and force the Southerners to concentrate their forces in one place where they could be surrounded with overwhelming forces and fully destroyed.

The Southerners wanted to prevent this, and thus attacked us unexpectedly with large cavalry forces in an attempt to prevent the encirclement. But the overwhelming forces of the North again fixed and strengthened the hole made in their ring. With slow but sure movements the Southern armies were pressed from all sides. Yet, on several occasions they were able to gather significant forces at a specific point and break through our lines, after which they made forced marches into Maryland and Pennsylvania.[2] As a result, they forced the Northern army to withdraw to a strategic location and change the fronts of the operation line or to restrict their movements.

Our mobile column marched out of our main camp in the June heat equipped with supplies for fourteen days and marched several days along the banks of the river whose sides were covered with towering forests that were inhabited by farmers. Here we encountered some kind of farm or living quarters, all of which were abandoned and destroyed by Blacks escaping from their masters, or by Indians who were, for the most part friendly to neither the Southerners nor the Yankees.

As I already mentioned earlier, the Indians were our guides and for rum and hot drinks they showed us exactly where to find the enemy forces. Our march was often slow and burdensome. Because of our artillery we often had to make a road through forests and build bridges

---

[2]This general description probably alludes to the Northern invasions of Virginia in 1862 and 1863, and the Southern counter-invasions of Maryland in 1862 (Antietam Campaign) and Pennsylvania in 1863 (Gettysburg Campaign).

through muddy rivers, streams, and swamps. We usually established a rest camp on hills in places free of trees. For ten hours we marched and for fourteen we rested every day because of the scorching heat, dampness, and poisonous vapors along the muddy banks of the river. Fever and the shakes immediately prevailed after our march from the main camp. Horses also began to weaken because we could not bring with us oats and straw. We had to feed the horses by graving them in valleys covered with high and abundant grass. But after eating this grass, the horses collapsed during the march and were unable to continue. In the end, having gone deep into the midst of the forest, the wagons broke down. On the eighth day we had to leave the heavy wagons at an abandoned farm and load the remaining horses with food, indispensable articles, and ammunition. The Indians were kept busy hunting to supply us with fresh meat. They scattered out through the area into the forests and left with us several older Indians as guides. Indeed, we had with us buffalo intended for slaughter, but because of these burdensome marches they became lame and thinner every day. Their meat became tough, hard, and tasteless. In addition, we were convinced that our planned march was inaccurate and ill-conceived. This resulted from the lack of topographical maps, and the lack of information among the general staff of the topography along our route of march. Yet, we could not withdraw. We had to go in the direction assigned us. The Indians, however, confirmed that there was no other way to draw close to the enemy unobserved, and thereby discover his strength and position.

During our rest periods, being bored and desiring to become acquainted with nature in these lands, I often roamed about in the vicinity of the camps. Many times I met with various types of animals like poisonous snakes, alligators teeming in the swampy arms of the river, and even with American lions which the Indians scared away with shouts and shooting. The Indians were not anxious to meet these wild and rapacious kings of the American forest. The Indians shot only to defend themselves from the animal, but carefully avoid meeting him.

One time, while chasing a large and beautiful deer which I wounded, I went unnoticed deep into a pristine forest overgrown with various kinds of parasites. Although I had a compass on a watch chain, in the approaching darkness I could not properly orient myself and determine the direction to camp. The Indian who accompanied me left me going in another direction, himself trailing two escaping deer like the one I shot and killed. Because of this, for two hours I wandered in this labyrinth of large trees overgrown with rampant parasites. Night came and poisonous snakes and rapacious animals were quite numerous. Therefore, I was forced to make a fire. Then, with great effort, having climbed on a large spreading tree, I began to call out and whistle and finally shoot. But no one answered me and a shiver began to go through my whole body once I contemplated by critical position. When leaving camp to hunt, I did not report to the general but left quietly, without saying anything to anyone. I took 24 loads of shot, several dry biscuits and a canteen of rum mixed with water. One could not drink pure water because from this water we got the fever and the shakes. We even had to add chlorine to the water in which we prepared our food.

My position was critical because mosquitos mercilessly ate my body. Around me various voices of animals, and noisy, shrill calls of night birds answered me in unnerving sounds. My mind fought with the possibility of either being saved, or dying of hunger or from the teeth or claws of wild and rapacious animals. Truly, he who has not spent a night in a centuries old American forest on the Missouri or Mississippi cannot comprehend what one experiences upon finding himself lost in this abyss. Our Polish forests are nursery or shrubbery in comparison with these forests of large trees overgrown with various plants and parasites.

Sitting on the tree between three large branches, and having yet barely six shots on me, I recalled that the Indian when leaving me said that he would come to my tent for the rum promised to him and that he would bring me a wild turkey for supper. With this thought, hope entered my heart and with it came hunger and the pain of biting mosquitos. I decided to climb down from the tree and make a new fire because the smoke would defend me from mosquitos and the attacks of wild animals, and at the same time it would be a signal for the Indians who assuredly would want to search for me once I was discovered missing from camp.

I immediately left my comfortable position and lit a fire which, with a bright flame, lighted several feet around my area. With the help of this light, I collected a pile of enough dry and raw branches and sustain a lifesaving fire. In addition, all around the place in which I decided to sit by the fire and eat, I burned the grass so that the poisonous reptiles and scorpions could not come close to me. Having done this, I sat down and nibbled biscuits, drank water with rum, and I decided to wait there until morning for the arrival of the Indians. Having eaten my meal, I lit up a pipe. Each hour seemed to be a century to me. I kept sleep away with thoughts of the homeland and of our fall after such a magnificent past. My thoughts drifted back several centuries and with emotion ran through the pages of our history. With pride, and many times with deep pain, I pondered over the prophecies made by the farsighted priest

Skarga.[3] Sadness engulfed my whole spirit, and thinking about the misfortunes of the nation, about the martyrs who shed their blood, and about the children of Poland, I completely forgot about my desperate situation.

Loud shouts and prayers to the Almighty Creator awakened me from these dreams. The first rays of the rising sun began to break the dark space of the wild majestic forest in which I spend a memorable night dreaming about the fate of the Fatherland and about her future, because it was only for this future that I had any desire to live. In America I fought bravely many times, looking death in the eye on the battlefield, which always has been and always will be the proper thing for a Pole to do.

Once awoken, I knelt to pray as my mother taught me and, repeating it with fervid love and confidence to the Creator, I convinced myself that a true and sincere prayer brings relief and gives strength not only to the soul but also to the body. With new hope in my heart, and with aroused energy, I stood after my rapturous prayer. Looking at the compass with confidence, I moved in a southwesterly direction where I hoped to find our camp. I had to act quickly so as not to be left behind in this wild labyrinth when the mobile column departed. Quickly I made it through the towering trees and the overturned trunks which lay rotting and decaying for centuries and were surrounded by lush vegetation. They served as nests for poisonous reptiles, scorpions, and predatory animals. Everywhere on my way loud parrots, monkeys, and various other foul greeted me in this wandering, but no where did I come across a trace of human feet or hands.

In this way, fighting and forcing my way through the thickets and the brushwood, after a forced march of several hours, I reached a plain overgrown with high grass and bushes. There a flock of startled wild geese broke my fervid pace. My hunter's instinct caused me to raise my gun, aim at the turkey closest to me, and shoot. The beautiful bird turned over on the ground wanting to catch up to his escaping brothers and sister.

Raising the conquest, I contemplated the proper thing for me to do. I decided to make a fire. I plucked the fat young turkey and cooked it on a wooden spit in order to have something to eat and kept the rest in supply because the instinct of self-preservation of man given to him by God shows discernment and thought about the future. I concerned myself with the execution of my planned intention. An hour later I sat by

---

[3]Piotr Skarga (1536-1612) was a Jesuit who advocated a strong monarchy lest the Polish nation succumb to the designs of her neighbors.

the fire and cooked this bird carefully, diligently turning the spit in order that the fat meat did not burn and did not absorb smoke.

Being busy, I did not notice anything happening around me. I did not notice three Indians coming toward me until they stood by the fire and joyfully laughing they asked me why I quickly escaped from the night camp in the opposite direction of the army. Noticing the Indians, and with difficulty understanding their broken English and Creole language, I nevertheless jumped with joy and in the old Polish custom I eagerly greeted my three guardian angels, who at that time seemed to me the most beautiful and pleasant of people I had ever seen on earth. One of them, seeing the roast which I had put in the fire, quickly picked it up and with the quietest expression began to turn the turkey on the spit and with a stick he cleaned off the ashes and charcoal from this tasty roast.

During this time of finishing the roast the Indians told me in words and pantomime that not finding me in camp at sunrise the general ordered them to search for me. The column marched on leaving my two horses together with a soldier in camp. He recommended that we catch up to the detachment. If, however, something bad would have happened to me, the Indians were ordered to quickly inform him about this the next night. The Indians followed my tracks and found my night camp. Not having found me there, they followed my tracks and caught up to me not understanding, however, why I went deep into the forest on the opposite side of our camp. The reason for my wandering was my little compass which, as it seems, was a fancy German fake and only a bauble, not a real compass able to serve as a guide for the wanderer in the forests and wilderness.

Having found out about everything, I wanted to go on immediately but the Indians insisted on resting and eating the turkey along with their provisions of deer meat cooked and sprinkled with an aromatic powder made from herbs and roots mixed with salt. In addition, they had a bottle of rum which my servant handed them for me together with roasted coffee in powder form and sugar, which served to prepare a delicious dinner for the four of us because the Indians had with them copper dishes for cooking. After an abundant meal and a three hour rest, we moved on and at sunset we stood together with horses ready for the continued march. But at night the Indians did not want to catch up to the detachment and I did not want to remain on the spot through the whole night. In the night the Indian who went hunting with me and then abandoned me arrived dragging two deer from which he brought back the skins and the best part of the meat not eaten yet. We made broth from them and ate everything. At sunrise we left and caught up with the detachment the evening of the next day. The friendly general was especially happy that I returned in one piece, and in the orders of the day forbade anyone to leave camp. He agreed this was a lesson from which I profited for the future. I did not venture again in the company of an Indian into forests where a European hunter would not find an exit if he got lost.

Several days after my return to camp, we unexpectedly came between numerous and strong enemy posts about which the Indians informed us. With the aid of our wild guides, we withdrew unnoticed in another direction through a swampy area to disengage ourselves from a situation in which we found ourselves incorrectly informed about the strength of the enemy and his positions. During the retreat I acquainted myself with the shrewdness and innate war talent of the Indians. Really, if it were not for our wild guides, our whole detachment would certainly have been taken prisoner because we were surrounded on all sides by an overwhelming force of Southerners. They anticipated our risky campaign, but did not know the strength of our detachment. Sickness decimated us. Every day horses fell and we had to pull our two small cannons with the remaining cavalry horses. From these 250 dragoons, after a three week march, there remained barely 50 riders. Hunger, thirst and disease were prevalent, and many people became sick from eating contaminated meat. Only biscuits, spoiled from dampness, pressed vegetables, pork fat, and a tiny bit of black coffee constituted our daily food. It was difficult for the Indians to supply us with game because of the closeness of the enemy, and the threat that they would discover our decimated reconnaissance column. Finally, tired, hungry and in rags we returned to the main camp. The only advantage of this expedition was that we could observe exactly the position of the main enemy force on the Missouri. They were convinced that an attack by the Southerners, given their position, was an impossible task. We wanted to cut off the enemy's retreat and take his rear in order to later join with Grant, who was moving from New Orleans at the head of the Mississippi toward St. Louis.[4]

In this march the Indians did not suffer anything and were richly rewarded. Several of them became my friends during this time and remained in our camp and were my guests every day. When they could, they supplied me and the general staff with game. For this we gave them tobacco, rum, biscuits, salt, powder, lead, and old clothes for

---

[4]Ulysses S. Grant was at that time commanding the federal forces besieging the Confederate fortress of Vicksburg on the Mississippi River. The garrison surrendered to Grant on July 4, 1863, thereby allowing his forces, moving south from St. Louis, to link up with federal troops pushing north from New Orleans. The fall of Vicksburg thus effectively gave Northern forces control of the vital waterway which the city guarded. Żychliński is quite confused about location and direction throughout this chapter.

which they were very greedy. Indians do not like Yankees and unwillingly serve them. They felt so much more affinity for the Southerners. Me, however, as a European and a fervid hunter who did not even fear the wild animals, they liked, and they showed friendliness, confidence, and even affection. They also taught me how to protect myself from the fever and the shakes. They showed me herbs and roots which, when prepared with food, serve as a preservative from the terrible ague and fever which twist the bones and muscles and quickly becomes fatal. They also taught me ways to protect myself from poisonous reptile bites. They gave me a kind of prepared grease which, when smeared on the face and body where they were exposed to fresh air, saved one from the bites of merciless mosquitos and even scorpions. The Indians would be the most honest people if not for their habit of drinking which made them into savages and robbed them of the personal dignity born into each man who is raised free in nature. Also, Indian women would be the most moral women, the best mothers and most exemplary wives, if it were not for their habit of getting drunk. Having once lost their innate feminine modesty and delicateness of feeling, they are destitute of all noble feelings. I also found that Indian women, the same as women in Europe, are vain, jealous, covet glamor, dress well, desire to be praised, and are shown homage and loved passionately because love in an Indian woman is egotistical. An Indian treats a woman with much consideration, but he does not burden her with work in the time she is to become a mother or while she is nursing an infant.

I saw marriage scenes similar to those in Europe. They usually finish with a beating of the weaker side by the stronger side because their human nature aspires by instinct for the ruling of might over right. Indians respect old men and women. The commands of the leader of the tribe are faithfully obeyed and executed. However, each judgement or more important matter concerning the general welfare is decided by a vote of the council of the whole tribe. I am convinced that there, in the wild state, the legislation is always based on the good of the nation and not on absolutism. In addition, one need not be surprised that civilized nations aspire to govern themselves by the will of their elected representatives and desire to crush absolutism.

The Indian tribe which I came to know better was not warlike nor wild, but had shrunk to 240 people. Sixty years ago there were 2,000 souls which the old people told me about. This tribe has gone through sad and terrible times, and mostly because of this they have decreased. They became infected by old clothes sold to them which came from sick or Europeans who died from small pox or other diseases which the Indians did not know how to cure because they had never experienced it. The Yankee culture forced this tribe out of its original possessions with the help of powder and bullets or the help of poisonous, hot drinks which enflamed the pure blood of these children of an active nature whom emissaries from Europe conquered. Presently, they put to good use these riches which the Creator has bestowed on this land that has been hidden for thousands of years from the eyes, hands, and legs of Europeans, and which Columbus with his genius and faith discovered.

From what I saw there, I am convinced that the citizens of the United States, as former sons of egotistical and merchant England, do not distinguish themselves with Christian politics in the presence of the former lords and inhabitants of the discovered lands. They did not trouble themselves to civilize the Indians on the basis of the teachings of Christ, but on the contrary, based on the laws of force and the principle of an eye for an eye they destroyed and poisoned them morally and physically in a shameful way that is disgusting to every Christian. It is true that the Indians, seeing themselves driven from their land and forest, committed abusive attacks and murders on the surrounding towns. As a result they risked blood and unequal battles with farmers or the military which systematically fought the wild and war-like tribes of Indians in order to quickly and forcefully occupy their land and populate it with the immigrants. Indian fighting was on the daily agenda during the early years. It is my opinion that Europe would contribute more to America and civilization if, instead of murdering the Indians with bullets and demoralization, it would systematically send whole companies of apostles with the sign of the Savior in both heart and hand to civilize their fellow man with love, and even more, build homes of God instead of factories, forts, and tap rooms.

What is worse, the European colonists make it impossible for the Indians to understand that the white people's God, in whom they believe and to whom they pray, has to be better than the gods and creator whom the wild Indians recognize, pay homage to, and offer sacrifices and thanksgiving gifts for things given them in abundance by the spirit of Eternal Light. I heard such an opinion from the Indians complaining about the Yankees. I repeat this here to show the reader that not all fault fell on the Indians. They were almost completely wiped out in the United States. In one hundred years there will not be any trace of these first inhabitants and lords of north-central America, if those who remain, as is happening now, become converted to accepting civilization from new arrivals greedy for plunder and profit, and protecting themselves and their egotistical aspirations under the sign of the holy cross, a symbol of the greatest love and sacrifice of the individual for the ennoblement of mankind.

Having in short acquainted the reader with my opinions and observations concerning the Indians, I am returning to the descriptions and adventures experienced in the army and especially in regard to the mobile column sent for reconnaissance of the enemy's position outside of St. Louis.[5]

---

[5]Żychliński errs when he indicates that he was near St. Louis. A review of Dyer's *Compendium* for the Department of Missouri indicates that the unit in which Żychliński served were never assigned to that area.

Chapter 6

Lincoln Meets the Poles

After the unfortunate march described in the last chapter, we were forced to abandon the plan of circumventing the enemy's positions, and instead we changed the front of the whole line. As a result, almost every day we had skirmishes in which I took active part.[1] I, myself, was convinced that the persistent cavalry of the Southerners was far better than ours. In addition, it knew the country which we occupied. It would often attack us, especially our rear and flanks, which it could turn with forced marches. It caused our whole battle line to stop advancing. However, in the end, because of the numerical superiority of our forces, and our predominance in artillery, we moved much deeper into enemy country. At that time it was already evident that in the end the North must win. So many more new reinforcements and supplies arrived from Washington. As a result, we possessed tremendous material means. Most of the Southern states were troubled by shortages of arms, munitions, and money. Furthermore, the armies of the Northern states improved with each day. They became, through necessity, more persistent and militarily capable. They proved themselves well in the ranks. As a result we had many more capable generals and officers of

---

[1] Żychliński's regiment was assigned to garrison duty in Gloucester and Yorktown until December, 1862. Although the regiment did see action at Williamsburg on September 9, it is unlikely that it saw any further action other than guard duty and some routine patrols. In December, 1862, the regiment was reassigned to the Department of North Carolina. It is possible that Żychliński's recollections of skirmishes and cavalry patrols dates from this service in the Carolinas, and not from the 1862 campaign in Virginia.

the general staff who had learned well on the battlefields. The Yankees no longer need foreign officers. As much as possible, they are removed from important positions because large numbers of officers from the various small German states in Europe were proliferating in the army, and I never noticed any agreement among them. Each of them praises his king, elector, or prince, and criticizes the value of the army of another state. I met the biggest argument between officers of the Prussian and Austrian armies. They had a mutual hatred for one another, and whenever they could they argued among themselves. Many times it was amusing to hear the Germans argue amongst themselves about the goodness, wisdom, and bravery of their rulers. Amidst the free air and the army tents in America, one often heard such disputes and heated discussions among officers from various armies of German states and principalities. I came to the conclusion that each German necessarily needs a king or prince to govern and drill him so as to allow him to quietly drink beer and philosophize fiercely about liberal theories never brought to life in his own country.

In addition, together with the Frenchmen and Italians who do not like the Germans, I came to the conclusion that the Germans would not take to forming a republic even if the kaiser, king, or sovereign prince so ordered. Feudalism, greed for foreign property, and conceit for their own culture are so ingrained in German society that the Germans will need centuries yet before the traditions of knights, vassals, mercenary foot soldiers, and forays on foreign soil which accompanied the age-old *Drang Nach Osten*[2] could be removed from the minds and blood of the German tribes. The Germans who believe that they alone were called by the Creator to cultivate other nations, and that they have to rule on earth so that there is but one shepherd and one flock. Because of the arrogance of the German officers we did not have sincere, friendly relations with them. Even native-born Americans showed them a certain kind of disregard, stating loudly that they only came and fought as for mercenary pay. Often they reminded the Germans of the mercenaries that the princes of Germany sold to the King of England during the American Revolution. England sent whole regiments of these German mercenaries to subjugate American liberties.

I recall here what general history teaches us in order that the reader has an impression about the private life of the officers in the army of the United States, in the hope that the reader will realize that in America the

---

[2]The term *Drang nach Osten* refers to the historical German "drive to the East" for room to expand and develop. Naturally, any such territorial gains made in the East would necessarily have to be made at the expense of the Slavic peoples, principally the Poles, who already inhabited those areas.

Germans did not possess great power nor did they behave properly in a purely republican society. The Americans know what they can expect from the Germans in time of war with England, which must occur sooner or later between these two rival merchant nations who seek to grab from one another the profits of overseas trade.

In America they also know how to value the good characteristics and attributes of the Germans. Consequently, they see them devoting themselves to work in the fields, and especially in industry, because the sense of order and diligence of the German nation is a model for all nations.

One day President Lincoln also came to our army on a visit.[3] Therefore, I had the opportunity to see this person up close and note his attendants and his behavior. The President himself was dressed in black civilian clothes with a top hat on his head. So dressed, and surrounded by a modest retinue on horseback, he visited regiments encamped in their tents. His retinue was made up of several delegates of the House of Representatives and the Senate, several modestly dressed generals, a few foreign officers from the embassies in Washington, and a few others. Everywhere the President was greeted with great fervor by the ranks. He conducted an informal review without the pomp of European ceremonies. Many times he walked freely among tents in the camp and in a friendly manner he conversed with the common soldiers and asked if they were suffering from any shortages and if they received everything that Congress had provided by law. He accepted grievances, petitions, complaints, and requests, and no one was prevented free access to the person of the President.

---

[3]President Lincoln paid an official visit to the Army of the Potomac in October, 1862, following the Antietam Campaign. It is generally believed that Żychliński's description here, and later in his memoir, refers to that visit. Military records indicate, however, that his regiment was on duty on the York Peninsula at that time, more than one hundred miles from where Lincoln and McClellan met in northern Virginia. The description here may refer to a visit which Lincoln made to McClellan's troops on the Peninsula earlier that year. On May 4 Lincoln traveled by ship down the Chesapeake, arriving at Fortress Monroe on May 5 and spending several days on the Peninsula. During this visit he was accompanied by Secretary of War Stanton, Secretary of the Treasury Chase, General John E. Wool, Flag Officer Louis M. Goldsborough, and others on an inspection tour of camps about two miles from Fortress Monroe before visiting Norfolk which had only recently been taken from the Confederates. It was probably during this visit to the camps outside Fortress Monroe that the meeting Żychliński describes took place. Lincoln also visited Harrison's Landing on the York Peninsula in July following the Battle of Malvern Hill, but he arrived there on July 8 and by this time Żychliński would have been enroute to Baltimore to recuperate from his injury. Carl Sandburg, *Abraham Lincoln. The War Years* (New York: Harcourt, Brace & World, Inc., 1967), Vol. 1, pp. 486-487, 495. See also Sears, pp. 89-92.

The army honored the President by having the ranks present arms and raise their standards at the sound of the national hymn. The ranks called out "Long live the Union and the Republic!" I never heard them holler out "Long live Lincoln!" Always with a shout in honor of the President and the Union, they greeted the person who, though so modest and popular, nevertheless represented the will of a nation of 40,000,000 people and an army of one million volunteers. Once, surrounded by the staff of General Hooker's corps, Lincoln toured a regiment decimated in battle and decorated several times for valor⁴ because in one battle it repelled a whole brigade of Southerners seven times with bayonets. He removed his top hat and stood bare headed while the whole unit marched before him. When the standard, torn by enemy bullets, passed before him, he drew close to it. Extending a hand to the standard bearer, he solemnly and with honor etched on his face, kissed the shreds of the eagle of the United States that was sewn on the standard. One could not see any decorations on the chests of the generals and the officers. Only a wide, three-colored sash hung over their chests with the embroidered eagle of the republic, its wings open, rested on the breasts of the generals and officers of the general staff.

How did this review of the armies by the leader of such a powerful state and nation, and by the leader of an army of 800,000 differ from a review of armies in civilized Europe? In America the spirit of freedom and equality was everywhere serious and powerful, whereas in Europe, with the pomp of a feudal atmosphere, reviews and parades in the armies were conducted with a certain stiffness and slave-like submissiveness, fraught with fright and a disheartening of the spirit that was always visible on the faces of the generals, officers and soldiers. In Europe each soldier shook from fear during a parade, and turned, as if a machine, upon a nod or a threatening glance from the general to the noncommissioned officer. In Europe, after the parade and review the soldier and officer raised their hearts in joy that this torment had finished. In the United States the President himself would not dare address a soldier as "you," but addressed the soldiers as gentlemen or citizens. The person of the President did not make on anyone an impression of fear, amazement or divinity, but they looked at him with pride, clearly and happily with the feeling that in his person they saw the embodied idea of freedom, equality, and independence, and as a faithful caretaker of the

---

⁴The "Medal of Honor," first authorized by Congress in December, 1861, was the only official military decoration awarded to soldiers by the government throughout the war. It is unlikely that Żychliński was referring to this, but probably to the fact that the regiment had received official recognition in the after action reports, the standard method of recognizing specific acts of heroism by individuals or units at that time.

constitution and the will of the new republic through the will of the governed.

During the President's visit to the armies, the soldiers made among themselves a little joke. Seeing the President sitting sternly upon a horse in civilian dress and top hat, someone said that as a former tailor he had on him better clothes than the figure on the horse. But the soldiers would cut into little shreds anyone who accused him of dishonesty, a lack of republican spirit, or a lack of feeling for freedom and civil equality. The honor of the President was important as the honor of each soldier. They liked and respected the President as long as he conducted himself like the President of a republic should. No one dreamed that this leader of a country of 40,000,000 people could even attempt to be an autocrat, or desire to change or amend the constitution, the foundation of which was laid by the immortal Washington.

I experienced such an opinion during the several days when President Lincoln visited our army, and I even went together personally with several Poles, as a delegation, to the President's large tent in order to greet him and assure him that the spirits of Kościuszko and Pułaski alone led us to the ranks of the United States to fight on the field of battle for noble ideas and to defend the freedom of the threatened republic whose existence our heros aided a hundred years ago with their blood and extended their pure and noble service to this task. General Hooker[5] took the opportunity to introduce me to the President, praising the courage of the Poles in battle, noting how they conscientiously fulfilled their responsibilities in the service and their fervid and sincere love for freedom. The President shook my hand and stated that each Pole possesses in his blood courage in battle, is a good soldier, and that the United States feels deep sympathy for Poland and will never deny hospitality and bread to her sons. He also asked us how many Poles were in the army and spoke with praise about Rosencrantz, Krzyżanowski[6] and many other Poles known personally to him. Later, as is done by Americans, he sincerely bade us farewell saying, "Good-by

---

[5]General Joseph Hooker commanded a division in the Third Corps during the Peninsula Campaign. Later he rose to command of the First Corps, and then became commander of the Army of the Potomac during the Chancellorsville Campaign in 1863.

[6]General Krzyżanowski had been prominent in immigrant Republican circles in Washington, D.C, prior to the was, was a member of the District of Columbia Militia assigned to guard the White House in the early days of the war, and served in the Army of the Potomac for a brief time before being sent to the Shenandoah Valley. Thus, it is entirely possible that Lincoln knew him.

Though the reference to Rosencrantz is not specific, it may refer to the officer who served in the Peninsula Campaign and may well have been known to Hooker.

gentlemen, after the war we will not forget to reward those who aided us to fight the enemy who desires to uphold slavery in the republic, and those who sought to preserve the Union as a strong national and unified whole." He spoke to us in English and glanced with a certain sternness at a colonel in the Czar's army who was apparently not pleased by our demonstration, because at that time in Warsaw the defenseless Polish people were already being slaughtered and the Czar was being severely upbraided in the American newspapers.[7]

In the whole festivity in the camp during Lincoln's stay, the officers treated the soldiers with wine and drinks at their own expense and the soldiers later treated their officers while humming national tunes. They drank and toasted to the health and success of the Poles. Music was provided by two Poles from Warsaw and some Czechs who played for us *Jeszcze Polska nie zginęła* ["Poland has not yet Perished"] which brought us to tears.[8] Later they also played the polonaise of Kościuszko whose melody included the words "Dwernicki is in front leading us to Moscow." At that point several Russians raised their voices and stated that the Russian nation desires freedom for the Poles and they consider them their brothers. They further stated that the Poles will help the Russians free themselves from under the yoke of absolutism and they in turn will aid the Poles to liberate themselves and to join again into one national, indissoluble body.

From those Russians who spoke there, several are still living. Two are presently influential generals of the Czar, but apparently they forgot about the brotherhood with the Poles and what they loudly professed in the tents. Presently they, together with other loyal servants of the Czar, harass Poles who are compelled by force to serve in the Czar's army. Such is Moscovite liberation. It goes hand in hand with Prussian liberalism in regard to Poland. There are beautiful recollections which remain in my heart after this bloody and burdensome war. While across the ocean I yearned for the Homeland because of the sad occurrences in Warsaw described in newspapers and commentaries boiled my Polish blood. Often instinctively my hand grabbed the hilt of my sword or my carbine when reading about these murders in the streets of Warsaw per-

---

[7] General John Basil Turchin was the only general officer in the Union Army known to have been born in Russia. While there were undoubtedly many minor officers who may have claimed Russian origin, Żychliński probably referred here to officers from the Tsar's army who were in America as observers and military attaches, and not as active participants on the Northern side.

[8] *Jeszcze Polska nie zginęła* ["Poland has not yet Perished"] was the marching song of General Jan Henryk Dąbrowski's legion which served under Napoleon I in Italy. Written by Józef Wibicki, the song was later adopted as the Polish national anthem and remains so to this day.

petrated by the hired assassins of the Czar. Murdered were my defenseless brothers whose only crime was that they marched behind the cross to pay honor to the loyal sons of the Fatherland. The people offered strong prayers to the Creator to save the Fatherland, and in churches they sang hymns displaying a strong love for Poland. The Moscovite savage could not bare these prayers or mourning for the sons of Poland whom he murdered. He fumed furiously at the thought of the political madness that Poles were yet dreaming about rebuilding their homeland and leading the nation to freedom, equality, and independence. Such ideas were prevalent one hundred years previously in the Constitution of the Third of May[9] which sought to introduce these ideals throughout the nation, from the cottage and the fishing hut to the palaces and courts.

I knew from letters received from Poland and France that the Central Committee[10] had already been active. Educated Americans of noble ideas and principles expressed true sympathy for the victims, and at the same time indignation at the government of the Czar who pretended in Europe to be a liberated monarch. They praised loudly the activity of the Central Committee and solidarity with the Polish nation. They confirmed, however, that the people of Europe were not capable of giving justice to the noble, subjugated Polish nation, and that the Poles should not count on Napoleon III or on Austria. In regard to England, the Americans rightly maintain that the government there is more selfish than even the Moscow government, and that the Polish government can never accept active or even moral support from England in the open battle with Moscow. Also during that time the Yankees, vexed with the friendly behavior of England in relation to the Confederacy, threatened that they would take Canada from England and attach it to the United States as revenge for England giving aid to the Southerners and also for the privateering activities of the *Alabama*[11] which caused disruption to

---

[9]This is a reference to the constitution passed by the Polish Parliament on May 3, 1791. The oldest written constitution in Europe, and the second oldest in the world after that of the United States, it granted widespread civil liberties to the population and is considered to be the greatest achievement in Polish political history.

[10]The "Central National Committee" was an organization of revolutionaries founded with the goal of regaining Poland's independence. On January 22, 1863, it issued a manifesto containing a call to arms which sparked the beginning of the "January Insurrection" against Russian domination. When news of the uprising reached America, the "Polish Central Committee in the United States" was formed in New York to maintain contact with similar organizations in London, Paris, and Warsaw, and to raise both funds and public consciousness in the United States. See Wieczerzak, *A Polish Chapter in Civil War America*.

[11]The *CSS Alabama* was a Confederate naval vessel built in England which raided Northern shipping with considerable success. Launched in Liverpool on May 15, 1862, it was finally sunk off Cherbourg, France, by the *USS Kearsarge* on June 19,

the trade of the merchants of North America. In addition, English ships constantly break the blockade of ports and supply the insurgents with ammunition, arms, and various war materials.

1864. Before her demise, she had been responsible for the sinking or capturing of 69 Northern vessels. Because of her success, the term "Alabama Claims" was used to denote American financial claims against England arising from that nation's support of the Confederacy. These claims were eventually settled in favor of the United States by an international tribunal, and in 1873 England paid the United States $15,500,000 in damages.

Chapter 7

Life on the Home Front

I was among those detailed from the army to the state of Massachusetts to recruit new volunteers to fill the ranks of the old regiments, which were usually decimated by battles, forced marches and diseases. Often a regiment numbered only 500 men on the battle line.

Some states already had great difficulties in finding volunteers, thus delays in raising new forces occurred. Often they sent unfit people to serve, simply to fill the ranks. Furthermore, the states did not provide the required amount of clothing and equipment. The horses for the cavalry and artillery, for example, often arrived on the battlefield so poor that the Secretary of War was forced to send trained officers who were known to be incorruptible and disciplined to collect horses and equipment from the states.

During this time I recognized many abuses by the state governments, by generals, and by high government officials which were committed for the purpose of cheating the treasury and the central authorities. Suppliers gave bribes to the officials collecting the food, equipment, and various supplies needed for the army and navy. One was able to cheat the treasury out of many dollars with impunity. One only had to come to an agreement and share the profits with the controlling authorities. Often the officers whom the army or the Secretary of War delegated to receive recruits, horses, and equipment from the states were bribed to look the other way with presents or a percentage of the profit. These swindles included accepting unfit soldiers and horses for duty, and poor clothes, shoes, supplies and equipment. Quite often the states paid huge sums to the corrupt officers in return for a receipt stating that the assigned number of volunteers or horses had been provided. They managed as well as they could in order not to show a decrease in the ranks and in the warehouses, both of which often existed only on paper. To do this, people who were said to have recently been recruited were often falsely listed as having died in field hospitals, reported as sick in the hospital, or that they deserted upon receipt of the bounty which they received on enlistment.

By these swindles and deceptions, many Americans showed extreme cunning which made the Russian and Austrian embezzlements committed during the war in Europe appear as nothing in comparison to what these Yankees perpetuated during the long, bloody, and costly war. Gold and silver strongly rose in value until $100 in paper money would barely equal half that sum in gold. Because of this, all articles increased in value two-fold. Our military pay was in paper money.[1] As a result, the highest military pay and wages of the officers decreased and it was difficult to adequately maintain themselves with paper money because we lost value from it when buying things and when exchanging for gold or silver. For an average horse I paid $300 to $600. For a modest officer's clothes, from $280 to $350. Every month I received $216 dollars, together with the extras, but this pay did not suffice in order to properly maintain oneself together with a horse in accordance with the rank.

There were severe fines for such swindles and frauds, and the guilty were sent to the gallows if the swindle could be uncovered and proven. But, the same thing usually occurs here that occurs in Europe, namely, they usually punish the small time thieves and culprits as examples while they do not touch the great and fabulously rich millionaire thieves, or they even release them after they pay off those who investigated the matters and who were the guardians of public good and property.

I found out personally that among us in the corps of General Hooker, the Secretary of War paid three times for the same ice loaded on five merchant ships destined for the wounded on the battlefield. Ice was important because it was used to dress the wounds, and particularly to assist those with amputations since the damp, hot climate quickly brought about inflammation and infection in the wounds and if they were not immediately covered with ice. The field hospitals were placed

---

[1]During the war, both the Northern and Southern governments resorted to printing paper money in an effort to pay for wartime debts. In the North, the green ink used to print these bills quickly resulted in the nickname "greenback" being applied to them. Since the paper money was only, in effect, a promise to pay, it was not generally worth as much as gold in actual buying power and led to inflation. Also, because paper money was very unpopular with many people, it was generally put into circulation by using it to pay soldiers. Thus, Żychliński's analysis is generally correct.

in tents where the sun's rays burned the sick. Such sultriness prevailed in the tents that without applying ice on the wound gangrene would immediately set in. As a result, typhoid and nervous fever ruled in the camps and those without ice could not be healed. Consequently, ice was a salvation and was indispensable for the army. Each ambulance also had to have its own ice room on wheels, and was supplied with ice every day. Even this vital item was made into a corrupt business because on the ships, or on the wagons, the ice melted as the result of faulty equipment. But, although it arrived frozen into the hands of the suppliers or the commissary officers, and proved to have melted when, after some bloody battle, it was suddenly needed. The treasury paid amply for this because in Washington they did not skimp on anything in order to bring relief to those fighting, especially the wounded. In addition, the public charity of society was great for the army, and especially for the wounded and sick as I myself experienced. I experienced this when I was taken to the home of a respected family from a hospital ship that docked in Baltimore. This family concern I described in a booklet that was published by the firm of Kamieński and Company in Poznań in the year 1862.[2]

Having arrived in Boston, the capital of the state of Massachusetts, as the officer assigned to receive volunteers,[3] I became convinced that recruiting offices were open on all the main streets and in tap rooms. They convinced people to volunteer for the army. The workers had no jobs in the factories and complete stagnation ruled trade.[4] Therefore, to save themselves from hunger the workers had to volunteer for the army where they received a $100 bounty which they gave to their family, wife, and children while they themselves went off to the army. Recruiting and trade were conducted everywhere, but some agents were ruined because they were either undercut by others or by the competition for people, food, and bullets. Further, the competition for recruits became so acute that agents accepted people with infectious diseases like ty-

---

[2]This is a reference to his earlier memoir, *Pamiętniki z wojny amerykańskiej 1862 r.* (Poznań: Nakładem N. Kamieńskiego i Spółki, 1863). The earlier memoir has also been translated and forms the larger portion of chapters 2 and 3 of this book.

[3]Officers and non-commissioned officers were sometimes detailed to recruiting duties when the regimental strength became too low, yet they would normally recruit in their home states. Żychliński indicates here that he went to Massachusetts. Why someone from a New York regiment would be recruiting in Massachusetts remains uncertain, although he could have been detailed as a general recruiter.

[4]There was a brief recession in the North after the beginning of the Civil War when Southerners defaulted on loans from Northern banks and cotton textile factories had difficulty obtaining raw materials. Within six to ten months, however, government orders for military supplies and the attending loss of workers to military service created very positive employment prospects for American workers.

phoid, nervous shakes, the so-called yellow fever, and vomiting. Walls, stones, and fences were filled with various kinds of lengthy posters praising the regiment and the colonel, together with appeals, assurances or exaggerated promises, and invitations to enlist in the ranks. Newspapers with long articles announced the news from the battlefields. In front of the editorial office, crowds of people waited every hour for the posting of the last telegrams from the army which were spread out by corps and divisions among the vast borders of these states where this murderous, dogged and costly war raged. All of this feverishly influenced the masses of the nation to become combatively ill-tempered and hate the Southerners. This hate increased daily and led to enormous measures.

During such moments I arrived in the town of Boston, and before long began to take to our corps the fresh volunteers signed up by the recruiting office along with clothes and various equipment. Our commission was made up of a doctor of German descent, a colonel, a native born American, and two captains of the regular army, a Pole and an Italian. They directed me exclusively to argue to the governor's representative to send the soldiers, their clothes and equipment as quickly as possible to the battlefield. They gave me this duty because they thought that as a foreigner it would be easy to cheat and deceive me. They also tried various American tricks on me. But, seeing that these were deceptions and fervid desires to lead me astray in order that I alone would be held responsible for the swindles and graft, I did the only reasonable thing possible. Having found in Boston a Polish priest in the Cloister of the Fathers of the Jesuits, I sought advice from him and he duly explained everything to me. He directed me to a certain Catholic clerk in the governor's office who was also helpful to me in avoiding the traps which suppliers and state bureaucrats set for me. He taught me how to behave and look after myself so as not to be cheated and led astray.

Also, several days after my arrival in Boston, by chance I met on the street a Jewess whom I knew in Jarocin and who lived in Boston. She knew me as a child. Her father was for many years a tenant on my parents' estate. The Jewess, who recognized me immediately, was extremely glad to see me and right away led me to a cigar and tobacco shop where I met Jewish acquaintances from the same town and from Pleszew. They offered me services free of charge, telling me, in addition, that many Polish Jews lived in Boston. They had their school [synogogue] to which they invited me for a service on their Sabbath to become acquainted with all of the "Poles." They referred to themselves as Poles so that under the guise of being Polish they could take advantage of the friendship of Americans for our nation because in each patriotic home in the United States one can come across portraits and busts of Kościuszko and Pułaski. Heaven grant that in Poland the same deep memory, honoring and showing gratitude for heros, is maintained in the hearts of the whole nation like they are preserved in Northern United States, and especially in Boston where Kościuszko once lived.

These Jews talked to me with sincerity. Best of all, they exposed to me all of the behind the scenes intrigues concerning the misconduct and frauds involved in selling clothes and equipment to the army. They also taught me not to be made a fool of by cunning Yankees. I was in the synagogue and saw that these Jews, who in Poznań are enemies of Polishness and Poland and the most loyal supporters of Germanization, in America teach their children to feel that they are also children of Polish soil and take pride in calling themselves Poles and not Germans. Because of this, and because my father had defended the Jews from the vengeance of the peasants in Jarocin in 1848, these Jews received me with much hospitality and sincerity. The peasants had gathered in Jarocin armed with scythes, pitchforks, and various arms, being alarmed in the surrounding villages by the national government at the time of the Battle at Ksiaz[5] in which the Poles gave proof of their courage. At this time, in 1848, secret agents incited our peasants and encouraged them to murder and rob the Jews. But the quick intervention of the parish priest and my father, who came by horse from Pleszew to Jarocin, prevented this massacre and paralyzed the plans of the agents, who desired by similar abuses and violence to bring about a state of siege in the Poznań region. During this time I was a young boy, a teenager, but I already was eager, sitting on a pony, for a sword and rifle to measure myself with the enemy. In addition, I remember well these happy moments when we thought the star already shone upon us. One does not forget such moments, and they remain deeply in the soul of each loyal son of Poland.

During the collecting of the volunteers for the regiment, I also became convinced that in our commission the army doctor of German descent and the American colonel were bribed because as much as they could they made it easy for the governor of the state to give for military service many unfit volunteers. Also, the numbers on paper during the trip through Washington to the regiment showed many deserters who, in reality, never existed at all. Each such soldier-deserter brought a profit of several hundred dollars because his bounty sunk into the pockets of the defrauders, as well as the money for his clothes, equipment, and supplies. They wanted to do the same with clothes, shoes, and various other requisitions, but here they met opposition from myself

---

[5]The Battle of Ksiaz was fought on April 29, 1848, between the Polish insurgents and the Prussians.

and the Italian, and no intervention nor envelopes filled with dollars laid on our tables could change our decision. We closely inspected each crate and did not give receipts for the goods until after they had been received and inspected on the train or ship. I myself did the inspecting and the accounting.

The governor and some state senators invited us to sumptuous dinners and suppers where they showed us kindness. But this did not help because we always remained cautious and adamant in performing our duties. In the end, the Americans, seeing that they could not make us into their own mold, tried to send us to another state where, in Cincinnati, we went through the same artifice and enticements. But there we showed the Yankees that we were neither susceptible nor willing to take part in similar shady dealings. Before long we convinced the utilitarian American society that in the ranks of Garibaldi there was no bribery, since with his letters of recommendation we entered the republican ranks with appointments. The Americans knew that as a Pole from a family of nobility, I treasure honor over life and will not allow shady deals. But they could not understand why an Italian, a son of a merchant of Genoa, did not want to take part in these embezzlements and accept envelopes with money. He and I only returned it to the governor of the state as proof that the suppliers desired to bribe us. In the same commission they treated us poorly so that in the end, bored with this, we wrote personal letters to General Hooker asking him to recall us. He called for our return to the battle line, sharing our indignation and praising the fact that we desired to serve the cause on the battlefield and not to make shady deals that harm the treasury and a society which was already groaning quite sufficiently under the weight of the war. We privately revealed to the general the artifices and deceptions and he warned the Secretary of War. But this utilitarian exploitation of the treasury was already so embedded in society that nothing came of our warnings and disclosures. On the contrary, we exposed ourselves to vexations, harassments, and rebukes as informers, even in the higher offices of the Secretary of War, where for a long time things continued to be conducted as they had been because corruption had already crept into the very government that ruled there.

During these several months of collecting soldiers and equipment in several states we had the opportunity of being in the company of American intelligentsia, since everywhere they invited and met us at drawing rooms and meetings. Therefore, I became acquainted with the social and domestic life in the United States. It is completely different from European life, but has in itself many good qualities worthy of imitation. Socially, women especially stand higher than European women and differ in practical education. They had broader and more liberal ideas, and at least do not marry for money. Of course, the unmarried women in the northern United States have complete freedom, whereas the married woman is restrained. She is under the tight control of public opinion and social conventions. She must try to give herself to domestic life and at the same time she must try to be a useful partner for her husband. She should not become, like costly furniture, a burden or temporary trinket who, in the end, will cease to amuse the husband and become old junk, at best a hindrance in the family hearth and at worst a nourishment for false devotion, intrigue, and gossip. These faults, rooted for centuries in European society, are proof that women aspire for a ridiculous emancipation. Namely, a government under the thumbs of women who, under the auspices of equal rights, exploit the weakness of the masculine species for the weaker sex for their own exclusive and egotistical advantage.

In America a woman attempts to bring about respect in the minds of men and at the same time become an indispensable aid and comfort in work. As a result she becomes indispensable to the life of a man with domestic food and wealth. She knows that romantic sentimental love, together with sensual rapture, wears away through years in each marriage. If mutual respect does not improve during this time of married life, one will not become indispensable to the other. Marriages based on the first sweet tenderness eventually become slavery and a chain squeezing both sides. Women living in Europe, usually with model ideals, are especially cold and indifferent. They seek other ideals or interest, thus, as a result, children from such a marriage naturally lose most and escape from the family nest without any solid foundation for a social life or respect for their parents. If they enter the world with such feelings, in the future they be neither good citizens nor parents because *"Czem skorupka za mlodu nasiaknie, tem tez i na storość traci"* [the way you are brought up is the way you are].

The ideas mentioned above, which I saw in practical use in married life, pleased me. I really learned to appreciate women who have a great sense of their own personal dignity and as a result are respected by men and not treated with disdain. An American woman does everything to become indispensable to her husband, and secure for herself not only love, but continuous respect. They raise children in a practical manner, namely, to appreciate work and to consider the father as head of the family who alone governs matters of estate. They always instill in their children the conviction that exemplary and obedient behavior of children for the parents only entitles them to expect from their parents help and property upon reaching maturity. In America the parents do not impede the will of grown children, but if they do not heed the will and advice of the parents they lose completely the right for help and property from the parents.

Often in America I saw that a woman, upon entering an omnibus or wagon and not finding there an empty seat, did not need to trouble herself because immediately several men got up and offered her theirs. I did not see a single man on the street or in a public place who addressed a woman going by herself or persistently pestered her like I often saw in Paris, London, Berlin, and in other towns of civilized Europe. Also, I never came across there such a shocking woman-degrading sight as, for example, in Hamburg. In the United States a woman is respected and this is also the reason for the kindness for women. She knows how to respect herself. Therefore, the laws there are strictly enforced in defense of the veneration and freedom of women. As a result, they can find defense and redress from these men who abuse the loyalty and feminine weakness, or assail the respect and female honor with disdain for her devotion or the shyness innate in a woman. Only in a country and society where a woman is protected by law from the abuse and disdain of a man can mothers rest easy. Where respect is given to a woman the law strictly and widely protects her honor, innocence, respect. Sons must also see in a woman a companion for life and not a bauble or toy. Such mothers can only rear their children to be useful to themselves, to God, and to society. But only these children, grown to maturity, can be useful and honest citizens of a country which respects their mother and sees respect and honor given them not only by father and husband but the whole society.

I myself personally saw up close how family relations are in the United States. Being wounded and sick from a nervous ague, I was taken to a certain affluent house of an American family in Philadelphia to be cared for and treated. Therefore, I could experience this delightful feeling of warmth and family-like environment in which a woman makes a pleasant life and ties the family into one compatible and moral unit. In intelligent company they like Poles with a good education and good birth. They trust their honor and nobleness. Therefore, at the beginning, I immediately had the complete sympathy of this compassionate and kind hearted family, which during my several week stay there considered me almost as one of their own members. I also noticed other cases and examples and I must bow my head to the home life of the American families.

The town of Philadelphia is very beautifully situated and inhabited, mainly by the intellectual and financial intelligentsia. Therefore, I could meet people there with more profound views and scholarly information. As a wounded convalescent, I had enough time to make numerous acquaintances in the town. I came to know many secrets of the family and social life. In addition, out of curiosity, I also went to the dwelling places of the poor and to the class of society living from physical labor. As a result I also saw the family life of this class.

In the home in which I found hospitality, help, and care, three sons served as volunteers in the ranks of the army at the beginning of the war, and they were promoted to officers. I became friends with one of them and we were wounded in the very same battle. But his wound was not significant, therefore he remained on the battle line. However, the father, mother, and three sisters actively occupied themselves by taking relief and help to the wounded for which they sacrificed half of their considerable income. There were many such families in Philadelphia. One competed with the other to bring aid to the wounded and to the army itself. From volunteer collections they sent various things, even candy in various transports arranged at the cost of the donors. After my complete recovery I left this kind-hearted family and went off to the front. Like a son, they blessed me, not asking for anything in exchange except to keep them in my heart and loyally and persistently continue to serve this common cause, so noble and indispensable, to maintain the republic. Mutual respect and friendship joined me with the daughters of these kind-hearted parents. Common sincerity, confidence and respect shown to one another was completely sufficient for us. The young and beautiful girls behaved with such tact and personal dignity around me, a young and enthusiastic man of ideas, that I had to respect them and admire their behavior. Often we took long walks through this delightful area. Women in Northern America do not hide their feelings but know how to maintain the limits of personal dignity in such a way that they never expose to a descent and honorable man feelings discrediting their honor and good name. A woman also knows how to defend herself from troublesome provocation. Her behavior and sight maintain strictly the decency of each harasser.

A great aristocracy also rules in society. It is the money and intelligence of the services, talent, work, nobleness of feelings and deeds, and even of birth. But the local aristocracy is harmless to society, yet not ridiculous. It does not harm the republican principles and ideas because it bases and restricts itself only to a private and social life, not public life. They judge people there by deeds, services, and abilities and do not impede anyone when the person comes from the working class, or even from the lowest class of society, rising over others. On the contrary, the higher someone rises from the lower social class the more he is valued because work there does not degrade anyone but ennobles them. The more arduous and difficult the work the more it is valued.

The relationship of parents to their children there is extremely friendly. After being brought up the children do not depend on their parents' help for accomplishments independent of the will of the parents' position in society. Gifts and financial help from the parents are considered by the children as an act of kindness and not an obligation. For this reason an unmarried girl, if she desires to marry without the consent of the parents, can do so, but the parents are never obligated to assist her. Also, the son, at maturity, can express his wishes, but if they do not agree with the wishes of the parents he loses the right to help and even property after the death of the parents who are not restricted by any law in administrating their property after their death. As a result, children respect their parents wishes and try to be good and obedient. At the dividing of the property they do not argue like in Europe, nor do they desire to disposes their old parents of their property as often takes place in Europe, of which unfortunately in Poland we often have so many sad cases even among the aristocracy.

In the southern states the relationship is different in the social life because the older son there inherits the property. In outlook, a woman is not as highly regarded or respected. As a result, married life in the family home is not so compatible or venerable. A woman in the Southern states is often only expensive furniture, a well dressed person, an idler, and a bad mother and wife. I do not know worse women or greater idlers than those of pure Creole blood descended from pure Spanish or Portuguese blood.

In regard to religion, there prevails in Northern America a certain liberalism, but in the family they value the study of Jesus Christ. They teach children the Holy Bible, God's Commandments and they regularly attend prayer services at church. Americans in general do not attach great value to religious forms and rites. However, they see that each person is a Christian and acts as Lord Jesus ordered. They like splendid shrines and value highly exemplary ministers who occupy an honorable position in society.

In the army we had ministers as volunteers, and even Roman Catholic priests who took confessions and administered Holy Communion to the soldiers and officers. I never saw where they ridiculed or mocked the piety. On the contrary, they highly valued those who were pious in the heart, not just the mouth. They abhor hypocrites and dishonesty in the study of Christ because the Americans do not recognize such things. Often it so happened that when going into battle I removed my headgear and humbly crossed myself asking God and Our Most Holy Queen for protection and the receiving of my soul on the Final Judgment Day. But this did not seem amusing to anyone. On the contrary, they looked at me with respect and admired this faith and loyalty of the Poles for the immortal religion. I carried on my chest a medallion of Our Lady of Częstochowa[6] and a scapular. Often bathing in a public bath or washing among soldiers, I removed from my neck this sign and Polish shield against danger, kissing it upon removal and upon putting it back on without exposing myself to laughter, or even to the voice of skepticism, from the Americans. However, they asked me why I did this. And when I told them the whole history of the scapular and of the picture of Our Lady of Częstochowa, and why we Poles are so brave in battle, then they saw in us the faith which can only make a lion from a small rabbit, and through which a subjugated nation can become free.

Roman Catholicism has already struck root deep in the United States of America and is spreading relentlessly there because society is morally higher than European society and sees that without faith and truly Christian religion there cannot be any society, much less a republican state where everything depends and rests on the love of another, equality, and freedom of body and soul. Feudalism, however, they say, was not a form which Lord Christ chose because his apostles brought the word of freedom, faith, and love of they neighbor, and not canons, million-man armies, and contracts for foot soldiers and vassals.

---

[6]Our Lady of Częstochowa is regarded as the "Queen and Protector" of Poland. In 1655 the armies of King Charles X of Sweden invaded and conquered most of Poland and forced King Jan Kazimierz into exile. In November, a force of some 9,000 veteran Swedish troops demanded the surrender of the monastery of Jasna Góra at Częstochowa. The Prior of the Pauline monks cloistered there, Augustyn Kordecki, refused and led a heroic defense of the shrine which contained a likeness of the Virgin Mary that was said to be miraculous. For forty days some 160 Polish soldiers, a few gunners, fifty monks, and a number of local gentry and peasants successfully withstood the Swedish siege. This miraculous stand turned the tide of the Swedish invasion.

Chapter 8

Poland in Rebellion

When I returned from my mission through the Northern States, General Hooker immediately sent me to the battle line and did not want to listen to my arguments that I had to be relieved of my duty to rush to Poland where apparently there was taking place a bloody battle with the Muscovites brought about by atrocities and cruel treatment of a defenseless nation. Naturally, I desired to take an active part in the uprising. From Paris and Italy I received letters from friends calling for my quick return as there was a shortage of professional and competent officers in Poland. Garibaldi[1] promised that he would send his son Menotte, together with his bravest soldiers and officers to assist Poland in her time of need. Nevertheless, our organization preferred to rely upon the sons of Poland whose service in foreign armies had prepared them for the main encounter with the enemy of freedom, equality and independence. In addition, the organization wanted the fervent Polish youth, imbued with their noble ideas, to stand at the head of the uprising because it was thought that they would bring with them the peasantry, and thus the whole nation would rise to a general call to arms, ploughing the land, cutting and harvesting the fruits of their manual labor.

When I lived in Paris and elsewhere abroad, people recognized my admiration for the principles of Kościuszko and my predictions that there might be an uprising. Therefore, they urgently beseeched me to return and assured me that the organization influenced the opinion of the country and that necessity demanded that Poles fighting in the ranks of

[1]Giuseppi Garibaldi was the famous nationalist who led the movement to unify Italy.

the United States return quickly to Poland. In these letters they wrote that Napoleon III and his brother, a prince called Plon-Plon, after the Crimean War, loudly promised to give help to the Poles, and they even indicated that Austria would not be opposed to forming an independent Polish kingdom as a balance of power with Russia, about which our famous writer Chojecki,[2] being from the circle of Prince Czartoryski, informed me that Napoleon III, in confidence, told him that he would give help to Poland because seeing Russia entangled with the insurgent Poles he desired to attack the Prussians who were then already contemplating the annexation from Denmark of Schleswig and Holstein. Napoleon wished to form on the Rhine a secure border against Germany, since by this he could establish his dynasty for many years in France.

For Napoleon, the behavior of Austria presented the greatest difficulty because it did not want to conclude an offensive and defensive alliance. But, as stated Prince Adam Czartoryski, Napoleon III had to overcome the misgivings of Austria by giving her a free hand on the Adriatic, in the Slavic Provinces of Turkey, because Austria at that time was already coveting Salonika, Hercegovina, and Bosnia.

In Washington, if I am not mistaken, there was published a very rational and interesting article in November 1862 in the *New York Herald* which drew little attention in Europe at that time. However, we Poles always followed each political movement of Napoleon III attentively and thus read this article and were convinced all the more to believe the reports coming from the palace of Lambert in Paris.

As a military man I felt the need to go to the Fatherland and deemed myself not obligated to fight in America when in my Fatherland the blood of my brothers was being shed and in Poland I should pay my debt on the battle fields. I contacted other Poles remaining in the army of the United States in order that together we could submit a request directly to the President to be relieved of our duties. But just then in Washington they decided to begin a full-scale campaign against the Confederacy. Consequently, in the state of Virginia, opposite Richmond, there took place a concentration of around 180,000 troops for the purpose of attacking the capital of the Confederate States. As a result, the Southerners had to withdraw through swamps and forests at the site of the James River and Fort Monroe as General McClellan did after a victory over the Southerners and the conquering of Yorktown.

---

[2]Charles Edward Chojecki (1822-1899), a poet, novelist, playwright, and publicist. He arrived in Paris after 1846 and maintained close contacts with many French magazines.

I wrote about this remarkable retreat in which our fellow country-man General Rosenkranz, also from Wielkopolska, distinguished him-self while being in command of the entire rear guard that covered the retreat. It was during this time that mitrailleuses [machine-guns] were used for the first time. Speaking of mitrailleuses, during this time it had been improved in Europe. Presently they serve as a terribly murderous revolver to support the regiments and battalions of infantry during at-tacks on our defense by overwhelming forces of the enemy. With sure effectiveness we even used balloons to observe the enemy at the siege of Richmond. As a result Europe cannot invent anything new. On the contrary, it can only learn everything from the United States because even in the time of battle we already had field telegraphs joining divi-sions and brigades during this bloody war.[3] I already wrote about this retreat and battles in the booklet that came out in Poznań in 1862. Therefore, I am not mentioning the details of the adventures. I am only describing my adventures and views just before my departure from the army of the United States to Europe to take part in the 1863 uprising.

I only found out about the outbreak of the uprising fourteen days later after a bloody battle in which I took part.[4] An officer of the general staff, arriving with orders for our outpost, brought me this information. From this moment my soul did not rest because it constantly yearned to be where the blood of my brothers was spilling. I cursed the hour in which I enlisted in the ranks of the United States where the allegiance and military honor, so deeply inscribed in the heart of every Pole, bound me. All attempts by my comrades to persuade me that the uprising would fail, that Napoleon III was not planning to help Poland, that Europe would applaud the heroism of the Polish nation fighting with sticks against the well armed army of the Czar, but would not ac-tively come to assist us, and similar and somewhat fair opinions and ar-guments, however, were not able to change my decision to return to the Fatherland. Therefore, every day I went to General Hooker and other influential generals to request a dismissal or a year-long leave of absence for the healing of my wounds at European waters.

In the end, seeing that I would not receive a discharge or leave of absence for Europe, I went to the general commanding the corps and requested sending me with telegrams to Washington as a courier where I desired to pursue my case at the War Department, or with the President.

---

[3]The American Civil War saw the advent of many technological advances includ-ing military telegraphy, aerial observation from balloons, machine guns and repeating rifles, ironclad warships, and a host of other innovations.

[4]The January Insurrection began, as the name suggests, in January, 1863. For an excellent discussion of its implications in America see Wieczerzak, A *Polish Chapter in Civil War America.*

As a result, I announced to the general that I must desert if he did not voluntarily release me because my primary obligation was to the Fatherland, and that my conscience ordered me to shed my blood in Poland, not in America. The general was a conscientious man, a true republican and patriot. Therefore, he did not mistake my straightforwardness, but put forth the argument that in Poland the time of liberation has not yet come and that one can only dream about an intervention to restore Poland. He advised me to stay and continue to study this bloody trade and not disregard the career which awaited me in the United States after the war. At the same time, he assured me that he would always give me promotions and awards if I would remain and not die in vain in the uprising, or on a Moscow gallows.

In the end, however, seeing my constant and unshakable decision to go to the uprising he allowed me to be sent to Washington in place of the courier. He advised me to get from the doctor a certificate to recuperate from wounds stating that I must go to European waters. Furthermore, the doctor must confirm this certificate because there can be no talk about getting a dismissal as long as the war continues, and even the President does not have the right to grant me this in accordance to the decision of the Congress.

Later he ordered me to give everything to another of the officers and go to the doctor for the certificate. I did this and having received it I was sent as a courier to Washington. I bid my friends farewell at a lavish banquet where we drank to the success of the uprising.

I stayed in Washington for several days handing over the telegrams and reports to the War Department. I submitted a petition on the basis of the doctor's certificate to be given a leave of absence for the purpose of recuperating from my wounds. In a week I received what I wanted. However, upon handing me the leave of absence, I had to give the word of an officer that I would not wear the uniform of the United States, and if captured in the uprising I would not refer to the fact that I am an officer of the United States on leave of absence. At that time the politics of the Washington government demanded that it have good relations with Russia because they planned action against England for aiding the Southerners. Therefore they counted on an alliance with Russia in time of war with England in Canada. In addition to this, relations in Mexico and the noticeable desire to bring into existence there a French-controlled empire were unwelcomingly seen in Washington where general annoyance prevails against Napoleon and Germany. They can only count on the Russians as a sure ally in Europe.[5]

---

[5]See Wieczerzak, *A Polish Chapter in Civil War America*, for the diplomacy between the United States and Russia, and its impact on support for the Polish cause.

I found out all of this from Count Adam Gurowski who also advised me against going to the uprising. He assured me that Poland cannot count on the despicable character of Napoleon III, and that Austria will never abandon the Three Emperors' League[6] and will continue to blunder in its partial and hypocritical politics. Count Gurowski was a competent diplomat. He knew the deceptions of Moscow, as did our country and its society. Consequently he immediately predicted accurately to me everything that later took place. He maintained that the dictatorship of Langiewicz was only a maneuver of the party of the Whites in order to paralyze the revolutionary movement in the nation and to create an armed opposition to the uprising with the idea of an armed intervention of the powers unfriendly to Russia. He knew personally Chancellor Gorchakov, and as a result he predicted exactly what Gorchakov would answer to the friendly note regarding the uprising sent to Russia by France, England, and Austria. They also told me this in the Russian Embassy in Washington where I had an acquaintance, a Russian captain whom I came to know when he was an observer with the army of the Potomac.

From Washington I went to Philadelphia where I stopped to bid farewell to my hospitable and very dear family, and then on to New York where the steamship *Saxony* was to sail in a couple of days for Liverpool. In Philadelphia they advised me not to become involved in a fruitless uprising, as they expressed it. This good-hearted family so insisted that I promise to return from Europe if I was personally convinced of the futility of the uprising. To assure that I would keep my promise they ordered me to leave there my indispensable belongings: uniforms, important papers, and my pay book indicating my salary remaining for the leave of absence while wounded. I had to personally collect this salary every quarter at the paymaster of the corps residing in New York. The regiment where I enlisted and entered the ranks came from that state.

In New York I found a public meeting called to give moral support to the fighting Poles. A committee became organized to collect donations for the purpose of bringing help to the wounded insurgents. Almost all newspapers and magazines wrote in a spirit very friendly to Poland and appealed to the Washington government to issue a friendly letter for the uprising against Russia.

With this impression I embarked on the steamship *Saxony*. On May 12, 1863, I stood in Liverpool where first of all I found out about

---

[6]The Three Emperors League came into existence in 1871. Since Żychliński penned this portion of his memoirs in 1882 he no doubt neglected the exact chronology and thus created this anachronism.

the fall of Langiewicz's dictatorship, about the rejected blunt note of Gorchakov, the ban on forming a Polish legion in England, and the sending of arms and munitions. However, the failure of Colonel Łapiński's[7] expedition from London and the internment in Sweden of this first expedition, resulting in the loss of the lamented Colonel Sierakowski,[8] made it impossible to continue sending arms and munitions from England. In London I also had a relative whose maiden name was Morawska, and who married an Englishman named Bodenham. There I found out some very sad news, and about their upcoming trip to Kraków with funds collected from the English aristocracy for the wounded insurgents. I also decided to go to Kraków. I tried for a passport in the name of Stonewell Williams, a correspondent of an English newspaper. I could not get to Austria or Russia with my own name on the passport because I had yet not settled accounts with the Prussian authorities where I was sentenced to nine months imprisonment for illegally leaving from Bingen on the Rhine after a duel with a Prussian officer. Just after the present Kaiser took the throne, I received amnesty but I had to serve a certain time in the Prussian army for which I had no desire.

However, at the beginning this could have been achieved immediately if there had been less belief in intervention and more in the strength of the nation which would have taken to arms if it had seen deeds rather than proclamations and grandiloquent promises from the secret National Government. Furthermore, if the nobility had given the peasants their own land, which these people for centuries worked with might and sweat, the peasants would then feel that they were also citizens of the country and would feel obligated to repel from their fields the enemy of freedom and religion. That this was not done was the fault of the Whites.

As a result the peasants remained neutral. Only in some areas did they support the uprising, especially the areas where the leader and the organization gave tangible proof that a genuine uprising desired to give the people the land worked by the peasants and introduce equal laws for everyone. Czardom took advantage of this fault and ill will and proclaimed the granting of land to the peasants, maintaining that the reason the lords had created an uprising and rebelled was that the Czar wanted

---

[7]Teofil Łapiński (1827-1886) left London in the ship *Ward Jackson* with arms and volunteers to aid the Polish insurrection. The Czar's agents were able to thwart this effort.

[8]Zygmunt Sierakowski (1827-1863) commanded the insurgents in Lithuania. Because of the failed effort of Łapiński, Sierakowski, being short of arms, was defeated in battle and executed.

to give the peasantry their own land and free them from the corveé. The Czar's officials and his secret agents spread this news among the people. I was forced to send many of these agents to the next world where they could agitate for the Czar and the enemies of Poland.

In the uprising I desired to introduce the discipline and order that I saw in the United States. I had the village people with me who hastened to the ranks which I led. It was only with their help that, from June to December, 1863, I was able to maintain the uprising in the Warsaw vicinity, an area devoid of forests and mountains, but teeming with highways, railroads, and garrisons of the Czar's armies. I often alarmed Warsaw by cavalry raids, and I fought skirmishes and battles in the vicinity of Warsaw. On the highways between Warsaw and Radom, Warsaw and Lublin, and Warsaw and Kalisz, and along the Pilca river were graves in which rested the loyal children of Poland whom I led. These serve as proof that a handful of poorly armed Poles had the courage and heart to stand against the Czar whom all of Europe feared.

In the units led by me, fought mainly volunteers from the middle class and from village folk. I can honestly say that people can be drawn to the uprising because morally they favored the uprising and hated Moscow. Also, my stern, energetic, and radical behavior did not please the Whites and the Warsaw street braggarts. Because of this I gained very many from the memoirs of these people who took active part in this unequal battle. At the same time it will soberly and justly judge the views of those who dared to commit to paper their accounts and observations for the study of future generations.

God did not give the one and same warm heart to all people. Therefore, only the zealots love the Fatherland, freedom, equality, and independence. Others are not as patriotic. Materialism ruled society in this battle for survival. As a result, there are fewer firebrand patriots in the Polish society. But Polish blood has in it something that always makes it more zealous than that of other blood. Therefore in it, the love of the Fatherland's soil, for the noble past, and for freedom in a purely Polish society will never dim. As much as drones are needed for a certain time in the bee hive, there can be much talk in our nation about renegades, parasites, and drones. It is necessary in each nation to label as criminals those who desire to dampen and cool the ardor in the hearts of the succeeding generation. These who like Mickiewicz[9] and others aspire to warm and excite this ardor in the nation. We must consider our fathers and pay them homage in this way like the former founders of our Polish

---

[9]Adam Mickiewicz (1798-1855) is considered the national poet of Poland. His poetry helped inspire Polish nationalism and patriotic endeavors.

eagle nest venerated Lech,[10] giving him life, raising him to the power of a divinity, and showing us in legacy our land drenched with the blood of its defenders and inhabitants.

At this point I am finishing my description of my experienced adventures and impressions across the ocean, assuring the reader that my thoughts in such writing were always concentrated on one main point, namely, a sincere and fervid desire to have a useful life for the Homeland and my countrymen. Because a person does not live on earth in order to egotistically gain profit only for himself, but to be useful to his countrymen and share with them, as is said in old Polish, *"czém chata bogata, tém rada"* [Whatever I have in my house, I will share with my guest].

---

[10]Lech was the mythical leader of the original Polish tribe.

Chapter 9

Exile to Bajkal and Amur

Once freed from prison,[1] I was sent alone deep into the country located on the boarders of Mongolia and Manchuria where I could personally observe the condition of agriculture, industry, and trade. I was, however, of the opinion that man should always take advantage of an experience to constantly learn. Also, it is his obligation to explain to his fellow man what he has studied, experienced and observed. Therefore, I have noted everything that I saw and experienced during my forced stay in this country because no one can predict when such a thorough report about a presently untamed and sparsely populated country, so rich in raw materials that it has before it a magnificent future, will become valuable to mankind, and especially to us Poles. Siberia is a guiding star of civilization on the vast Asiatic East situated near the Pacific Ocean and a large and overpopulated China where the strength of the laws of Confucius have, for centuries, maintained a continuously stagnant state which is moving neither forward nor backward.

The Southwestern part of Bajkal has a healthy and variable climate, and if it were not so highly situated above sea level there would not be hoar frost in June which hinders the farmers from safely counting on an abundant yield from their labor. However, the climate there is also advantageous to the farmer because the frost is not very strong. It continues for a long time during the winter, with the hoar frost becoming rarer in May and June.

---

[1] Żychliński claims to have been arrested for his activities during the January Insurrection. After being imprisoned he indicates that he was sent as an exile into Siberia. This chapter describes the economic and social conditions that he encountered there, but unfortunately sasy little about his life and activities there.

Also, in this country there are many thickly populated settlements along the main roads and rivers, and nestled in the fertile valleys sheltered from the northern winds. The country here, however, is mostly mountainous and is overgrown with large forests of pine, birch, fir, and spruce.

On the other hand, the southern slopes of the mountains and the wavy slopes of the hills to the east are not overgrown with forests except for the coniferous tree, which they call the *Kedrem*. In the cones of this tree grow a tasty seed with a nut-like flavor. In the valleys sheltered from the northern or eastern winds lies beautiful vegetation. The flora is abundant and varied with the most beautiful flowers, and serves as a nutrient for the numerous roe-deer, stags, and big wool goats that pasture there and provide the inhabitants with food, clothing, furs and rather warm skins.

In the hills to the south I encountered wild apricots and peaches, and in the hollow I often found bushes of wild grapes. However, fruits like apples, pears, and even plums could not grow there. Only in the area surrounding the town of Blagonieczynsk can be found wild trees bearing these fruits. Sometimes the human hand plants fruits because the climate does not limit human labor and thrift. Also, there are variously colored narcissus, tulips, and lilies in June, July, and August which greatly beautify the area, especially in the eye of the exile pining for his homeland. Botanists and explorers of the plant world can find a treasury which was until now unknown, and will, at the same time, note the diminutive size of much of the vegetation, much as our own explorers have found in the mountainous areas of semi-tropical countries in the untamed areas of central Africa and Asia. Australia and America have their own flora and different vegetation and often because of this these phenomena provide the explorers with some idea of the various evolutionary stages which our earth had to go through before it became as it is today with its enchanting ornamentations. In the forests, and particularly in the valleys and the rocky gaps which rise above the thousand brooks and little rivers, I came across various kinds of berries of unheard of abundance and of various flavors and both medicinal and poisoning qualities. There grow forests of raspberries, currants of various colors, wild gooseberries and bird cherries with black and aromatic berries, bushes of lilacs and little red apples with a tart, bittersweet taste. The rivers there are also covered with weeds and willows of various kinds which, every winter, form the main nourishment of the white rabbits which live there in abundance. The inhabitants, however, do not eat the rabbit. They treat his fur lightly and refer to him in the Mongolian language as *uszkan*. Thus, the rabbit's only enemies are the foxes and martins, and occasionally some wild cats. In Siberia also there is a tale that is as much a lesson. It seems that among a circle of friends a dog ate a hare, but this cannot be understood because there nobody besides us Poles hunt for rabbits with dogs or with a gun. The inhabitants catch hares in a snare or a handtrap, but only to acquire the very fluffy and soft white rabbit fur to make soft gloves, stockings and scarfs. Nevertheless, the hare is a disdained animal and a Siberian prefers to eat bear meat than hare which he compares to a cat.

In the valleys and forests near rivers the hunter encounters a multitude of hazel grouse hens, black grouse, and wood grouse. Often while hunting for these birds he unexpectedly meets with a bear titillating his palate with tasty sweet eating berries. The bear knows what is good in the forest, and he knows how to find and select the delicacies from amongst the abundant floral life. During the time when the berries ripen, especially the raspberry, the bear becomes less wild and predatory. Indeed, I saw Ivan Ivanovich, as they jokingly call the bear, nourishing himself with these berries, and with potato stocks, while in the same vicinity are roe-deer quietly nibbling the aromatic food, seemingly without a care that their main enemy was occupied nearby in collecting berries in his fat paws and pouring them with true gluttony into his large stomach. Many times I also encountered a bear so stuffed with berries that he had near him a whole pile of uneaten delicacies. During other seasons, when encountering this nobleman of the forest one immediately removed the grapeshot from his rifle and loaded it with a bullet, and the revolver was also well loaded because meeting this nobleman of the forest unexpectedly was attended with a greater danger than meeting the most demanding gamekeeper or forest keeper in Poland during an unauthorized collecting of berries or mushrooms.

There, while sitting on the trunks of larch trees upset by hurricanes, I pondered the riches of nature, sown with the magnificent hand of God, and through the pristine forest of Siberia noted how the animal world reconciles among itself the differences between natural enemies, the weak and the strong, the wild and the tame, and that people can take a good example from this harmony in the animal world by nurturing themselves with God's only gifts in the pristine forest of Siberia and not to think and aspire to conquest, riches and domination over others.

In the vicinity of water, in a place protected from the strong winds of the north, are usually villages and wooden houses built in a row one after another. They always stand with the front toward the street, that is to the road going though the middle of the village, and have large windows turned toward the South. Directly next to each hut is a courtyard with a fence which encloses a pen for sheep and a barn for horses and cattle. Behind the house and the courtyard to the South was a vegetable garden without trees in which, during the summer, grew potatoes, onions, carrots, cabbage, beautiful cucumbers and many various other vegetables which in our fatherland the thrifty farmers grow. In more than one garden in the vicinity I saw seedlings of tobacco whose growth and large leaves amazed me. In August the in-habitants harvested the tobacco, soaked it in clay containers, and once dried out they used it in their wooden pipes, which were carved from the roots of wild apricot or peach trees. A Siberian never goes anywhere without a pipe. They fervently smoke tobacco and even use it as a cure for scurvy. The climate is very dry, and because of this scurvy is the main disease. Curing it is very simple by eating garlic and wild carrots which grow there in abundance. In Czyta one can obtain frozen lemons during the winter, which are brought to Siberian towns from China through Kijachta. In the same way one can obtain frozen fruits during the winter. These are also imported from China, or through Amur from southern Manchuria.

The cultivation of tobacco in Amur, in the area of Blugowieszczyn, sometimes takes great efforts, but I did not smoke the poorer tobacco produced in the Nerczyn region and the Amur country. Siberia must have this article for its own use, and sometimes it is able to produce this important trade article for export. Behind the village, on the southwestern side, usually lies a plowed field, and in the distance from the village in the fertile valleys protected from the winds the inhabitants have so called *zaimki* [pastures] where in the summer the livestock graze. However, the cultivated fields found in the vicinity are called *pasznie* [grazers] which are often created from cleared out birch forest growing on the south east and western sides of the hills. Because summer there is very sweltering, and few rains interlace the heat, the farmers convey water to their ploughed fields from the elevated brooks and smaller rivers through winding trenches. Such fields are called "watered pastures" because at the beginning of the dry season if there is a drought, a time of weak growth, or if it is parched because of a scorching heat, they let water freely into the sown fields.

Meadows and hay making usually lay near rivers on the north side and sometimes in the valleys between the forests. Grass there is so tall, lush and abundant that a good haymaker in one day can cut five wagon loads of hay. Stack of hay stand in place. In the winter they haul it in sleds to the villages and the livestock is fed with it. A good wealthy farmer prepares hay for himself, usually calculating four wagon loads for one head of cattle or horse and one wagon load per sheep. Whereas the population is small, the regions are huge and the abundance of grass is great in the valleys between the mountains, on the hillocks, and in spacious meadows situated near rivers. Consequently, if the farmer does not dillydally at work and submit to drinking, procrastination and vagrancy there is never a short-age of hay. These foul deeds still occur daily, and are the basis for the proverb "Cooked pigeons do not fly to the table."[2]

Cultivation of the field is performed with a plow which pulls a harrow. At most, one need only plough the land twice in order to bring forth a beautiful harvest of straw and in grain. They do not use manure there to increase the fertility in the ground because regardless of how many times one may fertilize one's field with manure one always gathers the same abundant and soft straw. Grain was abundant, and the land itself possesses great ability to produce vegetation and fruit.

The main crops which are sown are spring crops such as wheat, rye, peas, oats and buckwheat. The latter of these is the most successful and abundant, consequently it is the favorite grain crop and the staple food of the farmer. Every Siberian likes either the *blina* pancake or the *oladzie* pancake made from buckwheat flour, and buckwheat cereal is prepared and seasoned in different ways. These dishes, together with sauerkraut and lamb, are national delicacies. On the other hand, the abundance of animals, berries, mushrooms, and garlic in the forests, and fish in various large and small lakes, provide the Siberian with abundant roasts and seasonings. From fresh or dried fish he makes pierogis, another national dish. In all, the Siberian has enough food, lives well, and drinks a countless quantity of the leafed *kirpiczna* tea which, in Poland, we drink in moderation. For this reason I consider it necessary to briefly mention here that this is not only suitable as *kirpiczna* tea in Russia, but the simple working people in Siberia, and indeed all of Russia, have this as one of their main foods and consider it an indispensable condition to life that is necessary to maintain one's health in such a sever climate.

The Siberians systematically select the tea bush at the very beginning of the development of the flowers. This shrub lives only one year, and by the spring only the stems remain on it, with its yellow leaves at the bottom. The Chinese collect these remains of the tea bush and put them in holes made for this purpose and they sprinkle it, in layers, with a sticky liquid made from certain kinds of grass and roots. They then trample hard on these by-products and stems to push them together. When this tea ferments into one substance at the bottom of the hole, they remove it from the hole and press it strongly in a way similar to that done in Poland when peat is prepared to burn. Afterwards the new bricks, after pressing, dry at a hot even temperature in ovens made for this purpose. Thus is produced the tea which Russians call *kirpiczna czaj*.[3]

---

[2] Or, "To achieve something you must do it yourself."

[3] "Kirpiczna" is the Russian word for "brick."

It is natural that in such tea there is a lot of tan but it is difficult to find there tans and fragrances. The Siberian cook breaks off, or with a knife cuts off, the appropriately needed piece of tea from the brick, grinds it into powder, and sprinkles it in a pot or iron or copper kettle and cooks it for a long time. Afterwards it is whitened with milk. Many times the house wife adds some kind of lard or butter and salt to it, and serves this to her family in wooden bowl as hot soup. In time of fasting, and among the many Greek Orthodox, instead of adding milk, lard, or butter to this prepared tea, the cook pours in a milky substance obtained by grinding hemp with a bit of water in a wooden pestle, or by grinding it with a roller in a clay bowl with a mixture of water and a bit of hemp seed. Thus whitened, *kirpiczna* tea is always salted, and is not despised like tea buttered with little rings of fat flowing in it. With this tea soup they eat rye bread or *bliny* or *oladzie* pancakes made from buckwheat flour and buttered with sheep fat, tallow or fat of another kind, or often with butter. Such tea serves the inhabitants much the same as gruel soup or *zur* [sour soup] and potatoes serves as the staple for Mazurians in Poland, and sour rye beet soup is enjoyed by the Ruthenians for breakfast and for warming up the stomach and the whole body. The Siberian sweats while drinking such hot tea like boiling water, and consume an enormous amount of this. After eating this way in the morning he is already ready for work and can safely hold out until dinner, and often until the evening, at which time he will eat his dinner or supper and afterwards drink several "*bludec*" [saucer cups] of tea brewed in a kettle or *samovar*. This is usually taken without sugar, and sometimes with a "*prykuska*," a bite from a very hard piece of sugar. By drinking this pure, hot tea, his whole body once again begins to sweat, and he takes pleasure in this nectar without which the Siberian cannot live. It is his only luxury, and also his main medicine and enjoyment on earth.

There are various kinds of *kirpiczna* tea. Usually the price of *kirpiczna* tea in Bajkal is between 4,000 and 8,000 kopecs per pound, and from 60 kopecs to one ruble per pound of leaf tea, which is equal to our [Polish] pound.

So, in Siberia as in Russia, tea is an indispensable article and main nourishment for the farmer and the worker, as it is for the mightiest lord. Because of this they say there that one drinks tea in various ways: the placing of a piece of sugar in a glass with "*prykuska*," with "*pryliska*," with "*prygladka*," and with "*prydumka*." This means that one drinks pure tea thinking only about sugar. This way of drinking with "*prydumka*" is the main manner in which these tens of millions of ignorant masses of people, making up this colossus of a national body which geographically is called Russia, and of whose expansion the civilized people of Europe justly fear, whose governments take these people lightly because they did not suppose that Russia could ever be reconciled with the civilized peoples of the large Slavic family, maintain themselves.

Returning to the description or agriculture, I call to mind here that there is very little winter wheat and rye sown in Bajkal, although in some areas, and especially in the Nerczyn region toward Mongolia near the Szylka river, and in Amur near the town of Blagionieszczyn, they could achieve tremendous results. There the snows do not cover the land up to six feet in depth like in other parts of Siberia. Because of this, the danger of smothering from the lack of air during the seven-month winter does not threaten the winter crops.

In Bajkal and Amur snow does not continually lay on the ground longer then four months, and never higher than the elbows. Even I survived the winter there, and because of a lack of snow in December and January one could only ride sleighs on the rivers. At the end of January or the first half of February, at the latest, the sun shines so strongly that at times during the afternoon fresh water from melted snow drops from the roof.

More than once I reflected over the hasty vegetation of the buckwheat. Planted at the beginning of July, it was already ripe and harvested within six to seven weeks. Fresh cereal and *bliny* and *oladzie* pancakes made from buckwheat flour satisfy the hunger and the gluttony of the Siberians within two months after the planting.

Also I often saw that on a well watered and adequately tilled field from one bushel of sown spring wheat or spring rye the farmer harvests from 16 to 22 bushels of beautiful grain. One good farmer can harvest 50 bushels of shapely grain from two bushels of sown barley. The usual, average harvest from sewing grain brings from eight to ten bushels of harvest grain even from unwatered fields. If it were not for laziness and drinking, agriculture in Bajkal could yield still greater advantages and more abundant produce. Employed there, mainly for the production of grain for sale, are the so called *Chachly* [White Russians] who were sent there during the reigns of Catharine, Paul and Alexander I. They, faithful to their tradition, see their riches and the labor of their life in agriculture and in work around the field. Tilling the field and raising livestock is their main employment. Other inhabitants work in agriculture only so much as need be for their own food because they prefer to be employed in trade, as wagon drivers, as handymen of various kinds, or they roam through the country as hunters, workers in private gold mines, servants, or are employed in towns and factories, as tinkers, as highly capable and skilled carpenters, and finally as adventurers seeking thrills, freedom, and adventures in the vast woods, forest and wilderness of this country. From these people I discovered many interesting things about the life of the uncivilized, primitive peoples of Siberia: the Tanuz, Hraczon, Rurat, Ostyjak and Gilak who still exist in Amur and still bow to the sun and even the bear.

The Tanuz even have their own priest. They came to Siberia from China escaping from the revenge of some kind of ruling lord there. They built themselves huts and also are engaged in agriculture. The Hraczon are uncivilized people employed only with hunting. They are the rulers of the forests and inaccessible swaps. Once they are near Czita and lake Witim, and later near Iruck in the vicinity of Kamczatka. The Ostyjak engage in hunting and fishing. During the winter they have their hovels in the ground, and in the summer they migrate toward the Arctic Ocean. The Hraczon, like the Ostyjak, use reindeer whose skins constitutes their riches and whose meat, along with fish, supplies their food. The Burat are former Mongolians who wander from place to place raising sheep, cattle and horses. Many times they have camels, hairy with fluffy coats. The Burat live toward Kijachta, Czindaton, and in the area of Czita. They are engaged in agriculture and sell grains, but they hunt and fish and are of the Lama religion. I was in constant contact, and even became close friends with them. There are yet a few of these uncivilized people, and in time, as with the Indians in the United States of America, they will completely disappear. European civilization is repugnant to them, and they in turn avoid as much as they can not only state officials of the Czar but the strangers who kill them with vodka, cheat them, and increasingly restrict the free space in which they live.

Grain is sold there by the weight or the pound. The government is the main buyer purchaser, buying very significant quantities for its alcohol distilleries, the so called "*Winnokorne Zawody*." In Siberia however the government itself engages in the production and selling of tobacco, cigars and snuff. Also, from the time of the development of private gold mines, the producers of grain found good buyers in the owners of these mines which employed thousands of workers who had to be fed daily. Also, towns buy the various grains for their needs. The authorities buy many crops to feed their prisoners, and the producer also has a constant customer in the army which obtains from government warehouses, at a constant price, flour and various cereals, cabbage, and green vegetables. The prices are not too low and always appropriate for the crops. Every year in the spring the price of crops depends on the price which the government sets, and what it buys to supply its warehouses during the winter. As a result of this purchasing, supplying, and handling, large amounts of money are obtained from the Czar's officials who are authorized to buy crops for the government. The farmers there are far less exploited than, for example, in Galicia where the large army of Jewish traders engages in trading grain without the control of any market authority or prices established by the government to prevent the exploitation of both consumers and producers. These exploiters sneer at the hunger of orphans and Christian families because, according to the commandments and laws of the *Talmund*, the Jews must only take care that they become lords of the earth in order that their children and wives not suffer from privation and hunger. Thus, to destroy, cheat and expropriate the non-Jews is a quality, or even obligation of each Jew studying the laws and principals of the *Talmud* in Galicia.

In Siberia the absolute government of the Czar has reserve warehouses of crops for protection of the hungry and the beggars. In constitutional Austria, and especially in Galicia, in times of bad crops and hunger we had to go for hunger loans and comply to the old proverb: "When you are poor, go to the Jew." He then goes to the *Talmud*, wipes his hands in satisfaction, and raises his eyes in thanks to Jehovah for he knows that each famine and disaster must quickly make him rich. He has legal equality with the Christians, and there are no obstacles to his executing upon us his laws and the commandments in the *Talmud* which are so clearly useful to the Jews and harmful for the Christians. Having reflected over the predominance of Jews over us, I have to come to the conviction that the equality of the Jews with the Christians will not be harmful and dangerous to us only when the Jews renounce those unusual and harmful laws found in the *Talmud* that are directed against our society, and if they return to the pure faith of Moses with his Ten Commandments. They will be hypocrites and two faced in our presence as fellow brothers. Presently, however, their religion and the laws of the *Talmud* that are rooted in their blood forbid them to consider us and love us as brothers, and because of this they use their equality not as brothers but as enemies.[4]

---

[4]In this passage Żychliński exhibits a very stereotypical anti-Semitism which was frequently displayed in Czarist Russia at the time when his memoirs were penned, and in the Russian controlled sections of partitioned Poland. In this regard, though individual instances of anti-Semitism certainly existed, it is important to note that prior to the partitions, when Poland was independent, it enjoyed a long history of religious toleration which led to it becoming the most multi-religious and multi-ethnic state in Europe. Indeed, the Polish monarchy and the Sejm had guaranteed religious freedom for centuries. When, for example, he was called upon by his contemporaries to declare Poland for or against the Protestant Reformation in the 16th century, King Sigismund Augustus responded: "I am the king of the people, not the judge of their consciences." This spirit of religious toleration was later written into the celebrated Constitution of the Third of May in 1791.

In Siberia the government itself takes care of the agriculture and facilitates for the farmer, providing, as much as possible, a profitable market for the fruits of his labor and exertions. Nevertheless, in Galicia the opposite occurs because of the shortage of industry and honest trade the farmer bears a great tax burden and gives back to the state the largest tax of blood, but remains defenseless in the face of the exploiters. He looks amazed and depressed when his own trains transport through his country foreign corn that is so much cheaper than his own. At the same time he looks proud and powerless as duty free crops enter his country from those countries in which they can provide crops cheaper than he can because there they have cheaper land, cheaper labor, and yet by nature much better land. They are not so burdened as we are with scourges of various kinds.

Can we, the farmers in Galicia, living under such conditions, raise ourselves and not fall. I will leave it to the Siberian farmer in Bajkal to respond, if he will acquaint himself the same as I with the present position of a farmer and producer in Galicia. I made this reference here deliberately in order to convince the reader that he can draw a lesson only if he wants to learn. From my description one can learn about the state of agriculture in Siberia and why in Galicia agriculture is declining and does not have any prospect of rising if the condition and relation under which we are presently living remains.

Adding to this description of the state of agriculture in Bajkal, I must also mention here that near Amur conditions for the farmer are yet so much better because there, up to the town of Blagwieszczyn, the climate is milder. Even the fruits and grapes grow there. The winter is bearable there and the snows are not as deep as in other parts of Siberia. Cheap and easy water communication by steamship and sailing ships to deep Amur from the Pacific Ocean and from America provide agriculture with the conditions to flourish.

During my stay in Siberia, several hundred German families voluntarily went to Amur from the depths of Russia at the cost of the government. They worked there in agriculture in the area of Blagowieszczyn and they made a good business. Also, from Tobolsk and Perm many families voluntarily went to Amur and worked in agriculture, and in the year 1868, at the market in Nerczyn and in Czita, I saw put out for sale millet and corn coming from Amur as a product of their own work. From the beginning, when the Manchurian borderlands were first occupied and populated by the Army without a shot being fired, these lands supplied crops and products to the people and to the authorities' warehouses. Today, however, they possess their own products and grains with which they can feed themselves and even export surplus at cheaper rates than are set in Czita and Nerczyn. Presently the ships arriving from overseas, and especially from San Francisco, Japan and China, sail deep into the country and find food supplies for themselves at the top of this majestic river. They even export some articles, and northern Sakhalin already feeds Amur and supplies flour to the Russian Imperial naval warehouse in Mikołajów.

This fertile and rich country also has a great future because the climate is even mild in the central part of this river which bends with a turn in the very center of the country in southern Manchuria. From Blagowieszczyn the Amur flows toward the North to the port of Mikołajów opposite of the island of Sakhalin. Therefore this port lies a good bit to the north and is frozen three months every year. This is a great obstacle for trade and communication with the open sea. The rapacious government of Russia, however, soon remedied this by the taking of this vast part of northern Manchuria, which lies on a sea with a port free from ice through the whole year, and is connected by train or to the navigable Sungar River, thus making it possible to connect with ports in Korea which are convenient, free from ice, and accessible to ships through the whole year. Let the reader take in his hand a map of this part of the world and he will become convinced that what I have said is supported and that, in time, it will be realized by Russia.

On the banks of the Amur stood in the countless forests centuries old Hardy trees, and even Oaks from which one can build a large armored military and merchant fleet in order, together with America, to rid the Pacific and Indian Oceans of the greedy English merchants who are so corrupted with materialism.

After the change of system of government and the granting of self-government to Siberia and Amur, the first bold leader of this country will perform what I noted above because I have already discussed this very often with the people. With a map in hand, with influential progressive Russians and farsighted patriots, I had to confess to them that it is possible to bring their plan about because they would no doubt receive assistance from the enterprising Jonathan, undeniably the biggest and most dangerous rival of Old Bull[5] in the Pacific and in world-wide trade.

Perhaps I have ventured too far into the future, but we Poles, through our long and dignified endurance of suffering, have a certain kind of clairvoyance and we foretell that Europe must emerge in time from this large rapacious national body called Russia. The people of Europe, dazzled with its monetary riches and million man army, with its

---

[5]The term "Jonathan" was frequently used in the nineteenth century and early twentieth century to refer to the United States, much as we use "Uncle Sam" today. "Old Bull" was similarly used to indicate England.

excitable social ideas, must undertake, as long as there is time and pro-
pitious moment, indispensable radical steps of caution in order to cut off
the legs of this giant who already stands with one leg resting on port
Mikolajow in Amur with its greedy sight turned toward Korea, and with
its other foot virtually resting on the Dardanelles and Bosphorus. In
addition, if it comes to terms with the civilized Slavic people, with its
hands it will capture the lands from the Odra and the Sala near and beyond the Danube toward Greece the whole half of Europe.

How then is the human strength in Europe able to conquer such a
giant?

Only God can crush it. But can the omniscient Judge call upon
physical force large enough to force the introduction of Christianity into
China and India where English buyers did not achieve this? And will
this not be possible in central Asia? Perhaps God Himself can also call
this force to abase the Germans and the English. Roman tribes, however, will join together in such a similar federation and in complete
agreement will live with the Slavic tribes.

Writing about these dispensations of Providence in the future, I repeat only what on many occasions I hotly discussed with influential
people in Russia, and even with scholars and experienced explorers of
human history. Whereas the peasant shoots, God carries the bullet.
Therefore, I also accept everything from the will of God. I am even
convinced that the idea of freedom and independence will come from
American to Amur, far inside Siberia, and then to the Urals. Siberia itself, a nation numbering ten million, together with America, can expel
the Englishman from the Pacific and Indian Oceans and conquer from
Korea part of Southern Manchuria.

Free trade at the same time was limited in Bajkal with China in the
exchange for goods going by caravans through Mongolia from the so
called Great Wall of China. China provided mainly tea, some silk, a
little fresh and dry fruit of various colors, India ink, wooden dishes like
bowls formed from hard wood, and a few pieces of porcelain. In Siberia there are several porcelain factories, and China clay, the indispensable raw material needed for the production of the most beautiful porce-
lains, is abundant everywhere. Also there in great abundance are steel,
copper, lead, silver, arsenic and other metals. These metals, and dishes
made from them, go to China because from there it does not pay to
bring any goods to Siberia by way of camel caravan.

Here I must recall that along the Amur, and especially its estuaries,
are terribly strong fortifications which nature itself has assisted. Even
today the island Sakhalin is already fortified and I can assure the English

administration that no war ship of John Bull[6] will be able to sail by water route to the port of Mikołajów and to Amur. In order to conquer the fortifications found at the very estuary of Amur on Sakhalin, and even the center of Amur, it would be necessary for England to bring from India an army 50,000 strong and lay siege for a long time, and still it would be difficult. As an expert I looked at the plans of these fortifications, which were at that time unfinished, and geographic maps of these places. I must admit that the Russians have capable engineers and the forts are well secured from an unexpected attack by an enemy fleet. Fort Ochocka is also well fortified, but there is much left to do yet. Also, this port is less important and if it were occupied it would not harm Russia very much. They were not afraid to show me the plans and charts because it was known that in Amur I was an adherent of Russia and that I hated the English government because of its despicable politics toward other peoples like in India, Africa and Ireland. As a former officer of the United States of America, I was acquainted with plans for the future. Therefore, I could well acquaint myself and properly recognize the whole Amur country and its relations.

Amur imports from San Francisco ironwares and various dishes, together with machines. Sometimes ships even arrive in Amur from Hamburg. They bring candy, rums, port, various wines that are usually adulterated, coffee, cotton, and wool products. In Nerczyn and also in Czita one was able to buy ready made clothes, undergarments, and footwear imported from America at a price that was not too exorbitant. They were much cheaper than the things imported from Russia by way of Tomsk, Kolack, and Irkutsk to Czita.

While personally conducting trade I had the opportunity to acquaint myself with this country. I can assure the reader that I bought many goods which got to Amur from America by steamboat up the Szylka River. In the traders' warehouses in Czita goods are found in great abundance. They were also much cheaper than Russia goods. For example, ironwares, various arms, woolen and cotton things were all so much cheaper. Also, goods like sugar, coffee, raisins, almonds, rums, porter, wines, various marinated things and pickles were so much cheaper from those imported through Irkutsk. But the Yankees sent their worst merchandise for, as they themselves said, the half-civilized inhabitants of Siberia.

They traded with China in exchange for tea various kinds of skins and furs, tanned and untanned, very many horses, various metals of all kinds and color, very much woolen clothes and fresh deer and bison

---

[6]"John Bull," like "Old Bull," was another nickname for England.

horns, various fats, smoked and dried fish, and significant quantities of smuggled gold for which the Chinese were very greedy and paid well.

I was personally in Kijachta three times to make purchases of large quantities of tea for the private gold mines. In the opposite Mongolian-Chinese town Majmaczin I also found out that through the steppes toward the Great Wall, 600 *wiorst* in length[7] and without water, Russia possesses its own telegraph communication. Every so often there are built post offices in the middle of the Mongolian steppes, in which Czarist officials, with several armed cossacks, force the Chinese to prostate themselves before Greek Orthodox Icons and carry the emblem of the Czar, respected by the servants of the divine ruler of 400,000,000 people in overpopulated China.

I also must mention that often I hunted on the very boarder of Mongolia in Jableczne Gory in the spurs of the mountains. I also went on trading expeditions especially to sell mares or trade coral beads for cattle. These coral beads are demanded there and used to decorate the weaker sex who possess flat noses and tiny slanted black eyes and are dark skinned. The coral beads are called "*Marzan.*" From time to time I met with a few Chinese border guards. I even entered into political talks with the aid of a translator or of pantomime with the officers of the divine son. From them I often found out very interesting things and especially how they view the power of Russia and how highly they esteem the white Czar and his army.

The border guard is poorly armed with a kind of a flint lock rifle, spear, and a wide cutlass of strange shape almost hanging from the neck. Furthermore, these knights of the divine son do not know any military drill except to spread out single rank in a semi-circle and with a shout to lunge forward and on command to shoot. This is similar to the Don Cossacks who do not aim, but shoot in a column haphazardly and say "*winowata pula popadziot.*" This means "the bullet itself strikes the guilty." When they are chasing the enemy Cossacks also shout "*Nieujdziosz!*" This means "you will not escape!" Not long from now the Chinese will also assuredly learn the following lesson from them: To be everywhere and nowhere, escaping yet to threaten those from whom they are escaping. The Czar can only manage such a loyal and very sensitive following by granting citizens freedom, an intelligent constitution, a free press, and at the same time he can easily allow 200,000 people enter Germany to pillage and forage. They know how to alertly guard against the movements of enemy columns and protect from encirclement their 500,000 man army, and are both able and

---

[7]*Wiorst* is a Russian unit of linear measure equal to approximately 3,500 feet or about two-thirds of a mile.

burning with desire to romp through rich German villages and towns. Indeed, in Russia they often think about this walk to meet with the French near Berlin and with the Italians near Vienna. Proof of this is the recently printed passionate articles of many newspapers which are directed against Germany, and between the lines against Austria. The Russians can not overlook that Austria itself entered the Balkan Peninsula by occupying Bosnia and Hercegovina and with the aid of Germany and England drove the Russian army out. Russia will not forget this slap in the face and desires to revenge it.

The boarder guard officers of Mongolian origin have said that they see the impossibility of defending themselves from the armies of the Czar if they would want to occupy their country. They have even stated together with others that if the Czar would leave to Mongolia complete freedom of confession to the Lama religion, and leave them to continue the nomad life to which they are fervently accustomed, they would not have anything against the Czar because their merciless Chinese officers, collectors of taxes for the divine son, fleece the nation whose possessions are only at the grace of such high Chinese officials.

Here I describe also the way of collecting taxes from wandering Mongolians in order that the reader would have some kind of impression of why one should not be especially angry to exchange his lot for serfdom under the Russian Czar.

A high official, surrounded with cavalry and supplied with a good quantity of bamboo sticks, goes from one tribe to the other collecting taxes. On the steppes this, in practice, means collecting a certain quantity of cattle, mares, sheep, or valuables. Exceptions are made for adornments placed on altars dedicated to the Lama because such an altar must be in each *yurta*. For this reason, during the time when taxes are being collected, which is usually in summer, the Mongolians conceal their valuables in a hiding place. They drive their herds to a distant hiding place. Along the border of Bajkal, they anticipate with fear the arrival of the Chinese official, and they drive their best animals over the border under the protection of the Czar. This high official, coming to the camps and *yurtas*, by force and by beating with bamboo sticks, takes what ever he wants, robbing the servile peasant and leaving him an official receipt for the taxes thus paid. Then he goes farther on with his guards in order to do the same with others, driving in front of him his collected herd or packs of stolen items on camels. If he finds buyers, he sells them. Here, naturally, he will not omit blessing the servants with bamboo if they give nothing or have very little to seize. These servants, however, humbly receive the punishment and request that the pious and eternal living Arch Lama quickly remove the tax collector from the area. He allows them to find the dispersed and hidden herds of livestock, and to uncover the valuables from the hiding places which went undetected. Stealing flourishes here as it usually does in Europe where the example comes from the top. Therefore, the tax collector finds there on the steppes of central Asia willing assistants. The only difference is that in Europe it is done in a civilized manner, whereas in Siberia the sequestering and auctioning takes place by primitive means without ceremony and without judicial order to pay. For example, it is very different in Galicia, with its county finance commissars who shrewdly know how to squeeze juice from the taxed in order that there are no arrears in the tax coffers. But I always have preferred surcharge, contributions, findings, payment orders and execution pallets with their revenue and fiscal regulations than the practiced gathering of taxes in Mongolia by the Mandarins of the Emperor of China. In Galicia they take the final cow, the final bushel of grain, and even the sheepskin coat for tax arrears. But the impoverished, famished people do not meet with blows on the heel with bamboo sticks when the tax collector finds nothing to sequester.

From this presentation of tax collecting by the Chinese Mandarin, certainly the reader will understand why the Mandarin fervently serving such a duty and literally performing their obligations in relation to their ruler, are proof that the Czar possess in Mongolia such warm liking by the nation and that in time of war with China he will conquer, with little exertion, all of their large country up to the Great Wall.

Industry in Bajkal and Amur is only in the beginning stages. It is limited to distilleries managed by the government, mills grinding flour for the government and other consumers, several government mines producing lead, silver, copper, and gold, several private gold mines, several foundries where they make steel and cast iron dishes, several glass foundries, two porcelain factories, three factories of fancy dishes, several factories of pots, and pitchers and bowls of fireproof clay. The domestic industry includes the producing of sheepskin and fur coats, the producing of simple, thick dresses, pouring of candles, extracting oil from the hemp grain and from other oil seeds, the making of bright rugs from domestic wool, weaving of thick cloth from hemp which grows there abundantly and exuberantly, the producing of chord and rope from yarn and from help tow and from the inner bark, dry and smoke fish, the making of simple footwear and clothing from skins and simple cloth and finally the making of baskets from tree bark and from the stamen of the wicker, the making of various agriculture tools from wood, the making by hand of simple furniture from sawed boards, the preparing of excellent and strong wheels, wagons and sturdy, comfortable wagons and tarantasses.

Above all the villagers are not employed in the winter in factories. I count this only to the domestic industry.

In these jobs the inhabitants learn so much more from our prisoners and sometimes from exiled criminals from the depths of Russia, craftsmen, usually habitual drunks, swindlers and first class thieves of a choice kind.

Here I will recall also that the Siberians have a great talent for building houses. I have not seen anywhere such excellent self-taught carpenters like in this country. They build themselves whole, enormous, storied houses and warehouses. It is only enough to show them the drawing of a house or even a church and they promptly and with unbelievable precision make the drawing given to them or a plan sketched with the estimated measurements. Also, they are competent wheelwrights. They make durable wagons, tarantasses, and carioles of various kind. They only have to be shown a picture. I even came across talented self-taught mechanics among those who manage the water mills. They build saw mills, grist mills, a thresher from wood itself and a grain crushing mill or press to extract oil and they made an excellent so called fulling mill for simple cloth.

From all of this I am convinced that in Siberia there is only a shortage of appropriate schools where a nation could take lessons and develop in Siberians the inborn talent so as to be able to process the raw materials found in such countless quantities in this large country.

There is already wealth among the people, and the desire for education is growing. With education comes freedom, the ennoblement of customs, and nothing can restrain the desire to join with the rest of the civilized world. Knowledge, however, has no nationality. Also, it has no borders or measure or weights. The desire of spreading education and creating with human will and hands so much more sometimes also pulls Siberians toward China and Central Asia where civilization has such wide fields and brings to the uncivilized people the love of one's neighbor and holy freedom, equality and independence.

Our craftsmen and manufactures who were deported there as political prisoners were very much in demand. They earned a significant amount of money, especially the carpenters, male and female shoemakers, good tailors, blacksmiths, and locksmiths. For them, Siberia would be a real gold mine if they wanted to settle there. It is sad, but I must admit the truth for knowledge and for love is the same holy truth that our insurgent element was often demoralized. And as a result thoughtlessness prevailed over reason. Immediately each one wanted to become a lord and act as such seeing in the pocket of a prisoner several rubles. Usually with disdain they treated the inhabitants as second rate citizens and behaved as they were doing them a favor. This was for money scrupulously and well paid. Often the Siberian merchants and officers complained about these faults of our craftsmen and manufacturers. Also, with this behavior they scared away many who were friendly toward us and paying good money. The government wished, with the help of our craftsmen and tradesmen, to build industry and handicrafts in this country. Someday the Siberian will be grateful to the Poles for the lasting groundwork which we provided, and for the continued development of local industry and civilized handicraft. To Amur by sea came craftsmen and manufacturers of various nationalities and adventurers who also contributed to what the Siberians will develop in their own industry and trades. Soon they will no longer need to import expensive and indispensable tools from Russia and from across the sea. There is much yet to create with the work of human hands in this country, but another form of government is needed there, another idea by the civilian, military, and spiritual authorities. It is necessary to grant freedom to society which, being free and less constrained in their thoughts, will exert themselves with all their strength to produce and to introduce in this country a civilization based on the principles of Lord Jesus.

On this I conclude this conscientious account of my forced pilgrimage through the wild, cold, and melancholy steppes and forests of Siberia with a sincere request for the reader's indulgence because truly this work was written only for the glory of God and for the benefit of the Fatherland. With this one thought I took up this task. I hope that our biggest enemy and opponent is not able to deny me this.

Index